Life Cycle Assessment

This book offers an itemized analysis of Life Cycle Assessment (LCA) for use in any processes, products, services, industries, organizations, and so forth. Various challenges faced during applications of LCA and its extension are discussed, including their benefits. Further, the book provides practical examples of LCA in different core sectors, such as cement and construction. Each chapter functions as a stand-alone unit within the book and defines its individual role within the overall concept of LCA.

Features:

- Covers Life Cycle Assessment (LCA) and future challenges, including practical applications as a climate change tool.
- Connects life cycle management and LCA/environmental management.
- Explains benefits of LCA studies for both internal and external purposes in terms of various impact parameters.
- Identifies different raw materials or alternate energy mediums for changing inputs to reduce environmental impacts.
- Discusses conceptual extensions of LCA, such as LCC, LCSA, SLCA, and OLCA.

This book is aimed at professionals in all engineering areas and in environmental studies.

Life Cycle Assessment

Future Challenges

Surjya Narayana Pati

CRC Press
Taylor & Francis Group
Boca Raton London New York

CRC Press is an imprint of the
Taylor & Francis Group, an **informa** business

First edition published 2023
by CRC Press
6000 Broken Sound Parkway NW, Suite 300, Boca Raton, FL 33487–2742

and by CRC Press
4 Park Square, Milton Park, Abingdon, Oxon, OX14 4RN

CRC Press is an imprint of Taylor & Francis Group, LLC

© 2023 Surjya Narayana Pati

Reasonable efforts have been made to publish reliable data and information, but the author and publisher cannot assume responsibility for the validity of all materials or the consequences of their use. The authors and publishers have attempted to trace the copyright holders of all material reproduced in this publication and apologize to copyright holders if permission to publish in this form has not been obtained. If any copyright material has not been acknowledged, please write and let us know so we may rectify in any future reprint.

Except as permitted under U.S. Copyright Law, no part of this book may be reprinted, reproduced, transmitted, or utilized in any form by any electronic, mechanical, or other means, now known or hereafter invented, including photocopying, microfilming, and recording, or in any information storage or retrieval system, without written permission from the publishers.

For permission to photocopy or use material electronically from this work, access www.copyright.com or contact the Copyright Clearance Center, Inc. (CCC), 222 Rosewood Drive, Danvers, MA 01923, 978-750–8400. For works that are not available on CCC please contact mpkbookspermissions@tandf.co.uk

Trademark notice: Product or corporate names may be trademarks or registered trademarks and are used only for identification and explanation without intent to infringe.

ISBN: 978-1-032-07402-3 (hbk)
ISBN: 978-1-032-07403-0 (pbk)
ISBN: 978-1-003-20675-0 (ebk)

DOI: 10.1201/9781003206750

Typeset in Times
by Apex CoVantage, LLC

Contents

List of Figures ix
List of Tables x
Preface..xi
Acknowledgment...xiii
Author Biography xiv
List of Abbreviations xv

Chapter 1   Introduction 1

       1.1   Life Cycle Thinking 1
       1.2   Corporate Sustainability....................................... 3
       1.3   Life Cycle Analysis 4

Chapter 2   Environmental Management System 9

       2.1   Background... 9
       2.2   Global Movement 9
       2.3   Necessity of Environmental Management System............. 11
       2.4   International Standards 14
       2.5   Implementation... 14
       2.6   Extension 15
       2.7   Rebooting 15
       2.8   Reduction of Carbon and Water Footprints....................... 15
       2.9   Reorientation 16
       2.10 Factors to Consider 16
       2.11 Sustainable Future 16
       2.12 Continual Improvement...................................... 17

Chapter 3   Life Cycle Assessment 19

       3.1   Backdrop... 19
       3.2   Framework... 21
       3.3   Goal and Scope... 25
       3.4   Inventory Analysis.. 26
       3.5   Data Source 28
       3.6   Data Variability and Consistency 28
       3.7   Validation 29
       3.8   Process Flow... 29
       3.9   Functional Unit... 30
       3.10 System Boundaries 30
       3.11 Allocation Procedure... 31

	3.12	Impact Assessment	31
	3.13	Limitations and Uncertainties	34
	3.14	Greenhouse Gas	35
	3.15	Acidification Potential	36
	3.16	Resource Depletion	37
	3.17	Land Use	37
	3.18	Normalization	37
	3.19	Uncertainty Analysis	38
	3.20	Interpretation	38
	3.21	Classification	39

Chapter 4 Life Cycle Tools 43

4.1	Life Cycle Assessment: Environment	43
4.2	Life Cycle Costing	44
4.3	Social Life Cycle Assessment	45
4.4	Life Cycle Sustainability Assessment	49
4.5	Organizational Life Cycle Assessment	51

Chapter 5 Guidance for Life Cycle Inventory 55

5.1	Life Cycle Inventories	55
5.2	Data Collection	56
5.3	Documentation and Review	57
5.4	Input and Output Data	57
5.5	Capacity Building	58
5.6	Future Outlook	59
5.7	Integration	59

Chapter 6 Application of Life Cycle Assessment 63

6.1	Life Cycle Thinking: Policy Makers	63
6.2	Attributional Life Cycle Assessment	64
6.3	Consequential Life Cycle Assessment	65
6.4	Integration and Harmonization	67
6.5	Industrial Unit	68
6.6	Small and Medium-Sized Enterprises	68
6.7	Corporate Level	69
6.8	Consumer Perspective	69

Chapter 7 Climate Change and Life Cycle Assessment 71

7.1	On the Horizon	71
7.2	Environmental Mechanism	72
7.3	Reduction Measure of GHG	72

	7.4	Carbon Sequestration	73
	7.5	Carbon Capture through Algae	74
	7.6	Ozone Formation	74
	7.7	Eutrophication	76
	7.8	Ecotoxicity	76
	7.9	Human Toxicity	77
	7.10	Abiotic Resources	77
	7.11	Afforestation	78
	7.12	Land Use	78
	7.13	Water Use	79

Chapter 8 Life Cycle Interpretation 81

8.1	Introduction	81
8.2	Identification of Issues	81
8.3	Evaluation	82
8.4	Sensitivity Check	82
8.5	Consistency Check	83
8.6	Interpretation	83
8.7	Critical Review	84

Chapter 9 Case Studies of Different Countries 85

9.1	USA	85
9.2	UK	85
9.3	Spain	86
9.4	Brazil	87
9.5	Switzerland	88
9.6	Indonesia	88
9.7	Czech Republic	89
9.8	China	90
9.9	Germany	91
9.10	India	92
	9.10.1 Building Construction	93
	9.10.2 Building Operation	93
	9.10.3 Building Maintenance	94
	9.10.4 Building Demolition	94

Chapter 10 Future Challenges for Life Cycle Assessment 97

10.1	Awareness of Life Cycle Thinking	97
10.2	Mitigation of Climate Change	98
10.3	Globalization	98
10.4	Integration	99
10.5	Exergy Assimilation	100

viii   Contents

10.6   Circular Economy 101

10.7   Carbon Capture and Utilization 102

10.8   Carbon Neutrality 102

10.9   Sustainable Consumption and Production 103

10.10 LCA in Higher Education 104

10.11 Data Inventory and LCA Software 105

10.12 Conclusion 106

Bibliography 109

Index 115

Figures

2.1	Global trend of environmental demand for sustainability.	10
2.2	Evolution of EMS over six decades.	13
2.3	Various input data required from tools for environmental concepts.	13
3.1	Extended boundary for life cycle assessment in cement production.	23
3.2	Life cycle assessment of cement industry.	24
3.3	LCT-LCA stages and application.	24
3.4	Life cycle impact categories.	40
4.1	Life cycle sustainability assessment.	50
4.2	Life cycle and sustainability system.	51
9.1	Application of sustainability for the construction industry.	95

Tables

3.1	Chronological Development of Life Cycle Assessment	20
3.2	Life Cycle Thinking When Adopted in LCA Studies	22
3.3	Material Balance for 1 Tonne of Clinker of 2.75 MTPA Capacity Cement Plant	28
3.4	Impact Categories	32
3.5	Increased Blended Cement Production and Its Impact	33
3.6	Comparison of Product Alternatives	33
3.7	Impact Assessment of Different Building Materials	40
3.8	Details of Four Commercial Buildings	41
3.9	Impact Assessment of Typical Commercial Building	42
3.10	Comparison of Cement Having Different Percentages of Fly Ash	42

Preface

Energy and the environment are two sides of the same coin. When we make efforts to reduce consumption of energy, then the environmental impact is reduced. We need to tackle the use of emerging innovative technologies, shifting to renewable energy, and practicing six "re-methodologies." That which we cannot measure, we cannot control. In the past two decades scientist and engineers around the world have made efforts to integrate social, financial, and environmental parameters to evaluate impacts on a single index in terms of sustainability. Still, we are struggling for clarity in implementation due to the variable parameters of different geographical locations. However, a number of life cycle assessments (LCAs) with extended tools, such as environmental life cycle assessment (ELCA), life cycle costing (LCC), social life cycle assessment (SLCA), organizational life cycle assessment (OLCA), and life cycle sustainability assessment (LCSA), have been developed and are now in use. LCA is not stand-alone tool; it is iterative and flexible in nature so as to assimilate various sustainable development goals. Building such momentum helps to accelerate progress towards reduction of environmental impacts and more sustainable use of natural resources, bring efficiencies in the use of energy, and minimize impacts on ecosystems.

This book provides insight into the concept of life cycle thinking at every phase of product and services, which helps avoid piecemeal approaches and wards off the concept of shifting environmental burdens. But one will encounter problems while integrating different parameters of environmental, economic, and social natures. The focus of LCA as a whole encompasses not only the environmental impacts but also social and economic impacts. It is an important assessment tool globally certified by the International Organization for Standardization (ISO) and accepted by companies from all trades and services.

The present book contains ten chapters. Chapter 1 defines life cycle thinking, life cycle analysis, and corporate sustainability. Chapter 2 describes environmental management systems and their benefits. Chapter 3 explains the four phases—goal and scope, inventory of data, impact analysis, and interpretation of results—of life cycle assessment and its methodology. Chapter 4 discusses five distinct types of LCA techniques. Chapter 5 highlights the Shonan Guidance Principles, also known as global guidance principles for life cycle assessment databases. Chapter 6 elucidates different applications of life cycle assessment. Chapter 7 connects the impacts of LCA to climate change. Chapter 8 delineates various principal issues that come up during interpretation of LCA results. Chapter 9 presents LCA case studies from major foreign countries. Chapter 10 identifies a number of future challenges for LCA.

We know that LCA is a science-based environmental managemental tool to access resource consumption and usage of electrical and thermal energy and its output in terms of emissions of gases, dust pollutants, and their local, regional, and global impact. This book will be useful to those hailing from all engineering

xi

disciplines and industries. I am confident that students of the environment or environmental engineers working within industry will appreciate this book in particular.

Dr. Surjya Narayana Pati
Director, NICE

Acknowledgment

I profusely thank Prof. Mathias Finkbeiner of Berlin, Prof. Guido Sonnemann of Bordeaux, Dr. M. Salahuddin, Dr. R. R. Khan, and Mr. B. S. Roy for their cooperation and help. I have freely drawn upon completed R&D work, project/status reports of LCA studies and published papers conducted during my association with the National Council for Cement and Building Materials, Ballabgarh, Institute of Directors (IOD), New Delhi and New India Cement Engineering (NICE) Consultants, Faridabad.

I would like to thank all my family members, my wife Pratibha, and my children Soumya, Swedha, and Swayam for their encouragement and patience while preparing the manuscript. I would also like to thank my family and friends for their cooperation and patience, especially during the difficult period of the COVID-19 pandemic.

Author Biography

Dr. Surjya Narayana Pati, Senior Consultant (LCA), Director, NICE, and former Joint Director, National Council for Cement and Building Materials (NCB), has extensive research experience spanning over more than four decades in the areas of life cycle management, environmental management, quality control, and project planning and monitoring.

A CSIR scholar and doctoral recipient in chemical kinetics in 1978, he has been a front-runner for incorporating the concept of life cycle assessment (LCA) in Indian cement and construction industry for green and sustainable development. He has been associated with several LCA projects. He was advisor to an LCA project on PET bottles carried out by IIT New Delhi. He led the NCB team that worked for Central Pollution Control Board (CPCB) projects for developing environmental norms for Indian cement, refractory, and plywood industries. He was associated with more than 75 R&D and sponsored projects. He has published more than 60 papers in different national and international journals and proceedings. He has reviewed several papers for the *International Journal of Life Cycle Assessment* (IJLCA). He was a member of various committees of the Bureau of Indian Standards (BIS) on environmental management and LCA subcommittees. He was a faculty member at different institutes in more than 50 training courses on different topics of environmental management, especially on LCA. He was also a member of several review committees for mega-projects funded by the Ministry of Environment and Forest (Govt. of India). He has guided several BTech and MTech students of environmental engineering for their project assignment. He also contributed papers to seminars and workshops on LCA organized by the UNEP and SETAC in 2010, 2012, and 2014 and to the International Life Cycle Management Conferences of 2015 and 2017. He has visited a number of universities and research institutes of foreign countries.

Abbreviations

ALCA	Attributional Life Cycle Assessment
AP	Acidification Potential
AQM	Air Quality Management
BAT	Best Available Technology
BDL	Below Detectable Limits
CBA	Cost Benefit Analysis
CCU	Carbon Capture and Utilization
CE	Circular Economy
CLCA	Consequential Life Cycle Assessment
CML	Leiden University Institute of Environmental Sciences
COP	Conference of the Parties (to the United Nations Framework Convention on Climate Change)
CPP	Captive Power Plant
CT	Clean Technology
DFE	Design for Environment
EAu	Environment Audit
EC	European Commission
EEA	European Environment Agency
EIA	Environmental Impact Assessment
ELCA	Environmental Life Cycle Assessment
EMA	Energy Material Analysis
EMP	Environmental Management Planning
EMS	Environmental Management System
EPD	Environmental Product Declaration
EPE	Environmental Performance Evaluation
ER	Environmental Risk
ERA	Environmental Risk Assessment
EU	European Union
GHG	Greenhouse Gas
GWI	Global Warming Index
GWP	Global Warming Potential
HRA	Health Risk Assessment
HT	Human Toxicity
IE	Industrial Ecology
IEA	International Energy Agency
IJLCA	*International Journal of Life Cycle Assessment*
ILCD	International Reference Life Cycle Data System
IPCC	Intergovernmental Panel on Climate Change
ISCM	Integrated Substance Chain Management
ISO	International Organization for Standardization
IVL	Swedish Environmental Research Institute

LCA	Life Cycle Assessment
LCC	Life Cycle Costing
LCI	Life Cycle Inventory
LCIA	Life Cycle Impact Assessment
LCM	Life Cycle Management
LCSA	Life Cycle Sustainability Assessment
LCT	Life Cycle Thinking
LUC	Land Use Change
MIC	Methyl Isocyanate
NCB	National Council for Cement and Building Materials
NGO	Non-Governmental Organization
ODS	Ozone-Depleting Substances
OLCA	Organizational Life Cycle Assessment
PLA	Product Line Analysis
R&D	Research and Development
SDGs	Sustainable Development Goals
SETAC	Society of Environmental Toxicology and Chemistry
SFA	Substance Flow Analysis
SLCA	Social Life Cycle Assessment
SMEs	Small and Medium-Sized Enterprises
TQEM	Total Quality Environmental Management
UNEP	United Nations Environment Programme
US	EPA United States Environmental Protection Agency
WBCSD	World Business Council for Sustainable Development
WCED	World Commission on Environment and Development
WRI	World Resources Institute

1 Introduction

The environment is not a new concept, in its current incarnation. It might be novel, but its roots are ancient and global in nature. The majority of early civilization lived in remarkably close proximity to and in harmony with nature. In all philosophy, worship of nature is part of daily life. In Sanātana Dharma, Jainism, Buddhism, Taoism, Confucianism, and for Native Americans and other tribes, the importance of striving for balance and living in respect of and harmony with nature has been emphasized. However, it seems that these philosophies have not carried over into contemporary mainstreams, due to modern lifestyles. In recent years, the concept of the environment has taken on a never-before-seen sense of urgency as we have witnessed the degradation of forests and massive global industrialization on unprecedented scales.

In the process of industrial and economic progress, how to achieve the goal of harmonious development between society and industries is an important issue not only for governments but also for the whole world and its ecosystems. In the last one and half centuries, most of our industrial activities have wreaked havoc on nature. But in the 1960s and 1970s, the industrial world recognized the gigantic environmental problem and the need for its abatement. Given the problems of environmental pollution and energy consumption and intensification of resource exhaustion, governments and international organizations have been rethinking and working seriously to determine what kind of role enterprise should play in the process of social development. The biggest threat to humanity is climate change; rising temperatures have caused melting ice peaks, forest fires, inundation of low lying sea coast, rise of sea levels, uneven precipitation in turn causing isolated sporadic heavy rains and flooding of cities, overflowing of rivers and frequent landslides, and other natural calamities around the world.

As an important component of society, enterprises have caused numerous environmental problems due to consumption of various raw materials and thermal and electrical energy resources for manufacturing different products or services. Therefore, companies should not only operate in pursuit of profit but also take on social responsibilities by serving various stakeholders such as the government, community, customers, and employees and paying attention to the safety of their products, processes, and their impact on the environment. The public has the right to know about the social responsibility performance of companies, and government is strengthening regulations on the environment and corporate social responsibility disclosures.

1.1 LIFE CYCLE THINKING

Life cycle thinking (LCT) is essential for forging a path to sustainability by expanding the focus on the production site to the whole product life cycle, which

DOI: 10.1201/9781003206750-1

facilitates links between economic and environmental dimensions within an organization. Life cycle thinking is about widening views to expand the traditional focus on manufacturing processes to incorporate various aspects associated with products over their entire life cycle. The producer becomes responsible for the product from the cradle to grave and must, for instance, develop products with improved performance in all phases of the product life cycle. The main goal of product LCT is to reduce resource use and emissions as well as improve social performance in various stages of a product's life. In this way, companies achieve cleaner products and processes, a competitive advantage in the marketplace, and more sustainable business practices.

LCT philosophy will be useful in future business practices. It is based on the principle of pollution prevention where environmental impacts are reduced at the source itself. These principles have so far been implemented internally in organizations via cleaner production, best available technology (BAT), and adapting environmental management systems (EMSs). LCT expands the concept of pollution prevention to include the whole product life cycle and sustainability. Sources of reduction are achieved by adapting a circular economy (CE) through the "Six Re-philosophy":

1. *Re*thinking the product and its function. For example, the product may be used more efficiently, thereby reducing energy use and other natural resources.
2. *Re*ducing energy and material used throughout the product life cycle.
3. *Re*placing harmful substances with more environmentally friendly alternatives.
4. *Re*cycling select materials that can be easily recycled and used to build the product.
5. *Re*using parts of the product to create new products.
6. *Re*pairing the product instead of replacing it, and designing the product so it is easy to repair.

In each life cycle stage, there is the potential to lower resource consumption and improve the performance of products. It is an iterative process.

The concept of corporate sustainability originates from the broader concept of sustainability, which itself was shaped through several NGOs and public and academic influences over time, including the sustainability movement of the early 21st century. The environmental counter technology movement in 1960s and 1970s the "No growth" philosophy which emerged in 1970s as well as contribution from the discipline of ecology. During 1980s, social issues became more prominent, including human rights the quality of life as well as poverty elevation, especially in less developed countries. Public pressure increased for new approaches to environment and development and to integrate Environmental Protection with a development that would ultimately lead to an elevation of poverty. The definition of sustainability became known on a global level through the report by the Brundtland Commission, formerly the World

Introduction 3

Commission on the Environment and Development (WCED, 1987), an entity of the United Nations.

The WCED related sustainability to environmental integrity and social equity, but also to corporations and economic prosperity by coining the term *sustainable development*, defined as "development that meets the needs of present without compromising the ability of future generations to meet their own needs" (WCED, 1987, p. 43). The 1992 Earth Summit in Rio de Janeiro resulted in widespread acceptance of this definition by business leaders, politicians, and NGOs. For organizations, it implied the challenge to simultaneously improve social and human welfare while reducing their ecological impact and ensuring the effective achievement of organizational objectives. Based on the WCED definition, as well as on influence from strategy and management planners, a variety of subsequent definitions of sustainability emerged in relation to organizations, in particular corporate sustainability.

1.2 CORPORATE SUSTAINABILITY

The concept of corporate sustainability has gained importance in recent years in both organizational policies as well as practices. While there still exists a lack of clarity on what constitutes corporate sustainability and how to best achieve it, many scientists and management scholars suggest that the pathway for adaptation of corporate sustainability principles leads out of the adaptation of a sustainability-oriented organizational culture. In a closer examination by various school of thoughts it has been observed that there is an intrinsic bond or link between the cultural orientation of an organization and pursuit of corporate sustainability principles. In recent years, many organizations have introduced or changed policies, products, and/or processes to address pollution, minimize resources and energy consumption, and improve community and stakeholder relations. Several scholars, however, maintain that these changes are insufficient, superficial, and not conducive to the formation of sustainable organizations and industries on a large scale. It has been argued that to respond to environmental and social challenges organizations will have to undergo significant cultural changes and transformations. The central idea is that organizations will have to develop a sustainability-oriented organizational culture when moving towards corporate sustainability.

We are aware that corporate sustainability is a term that doesn't stand alone. It relates to growth of the corporation in a situation where the corporation ensures both growth of society and protection of the environment. A new term now in vogue is *sustainable green development*. Sustainability management theory has always emphasized supporting climate change and percolating sustainability into organizations. The assumption is that companies in which top management takes interest in these issues can manage them consistently. The key to successful governance is translating sustainability performance improvement goals into executive targets. An integrated approach and an emphasis on sustainability becomes necessary because of the complexity, crucial linkages, and vast interrelation found in the problem of managing fragile resources and energy and expanding

4 Life Cycle Assessment

populations. The desired balance and holistic approaches as well as sustainable development are an expression of global efforts to balance all resources, populations, and cultures and to overcome traditional industrial models of rapid growth and higher profitability.

Sustainable development can become an alternative concept in providing for a viable environment and protection of ecosystems. In attempting to avoid total degradation, there is an emphasis on global interdependence and a conscious effort to avoid drifts towards catastrophe. In order to implement this development in corporations, there needs to be a committed chief sustainability officer. In subsequent chapters, tools like life cycle assessment, required to achieve sustainability, are discussed in detail and the essential components of sustainability are outlined. It is a compelling vision of a sustainable future, building goals and targets for all levels of the organization. Reversing what is unsustainable requires innovative measures consistent with a vision of a pathway to sustainability and must be accompanied by identifying and reversing unsustainable policy. Applying leverage, a corporation will have a successful transition using an array of measures that strengthen its sustainability mindset throughout the organization by raising awareness and educating all stakeholders. This is also achievable by changing the rules regarding incentives to advance sustainable practices in day-to-day activities. Adaptive management and governance need capacity to manage process through continuous monitoring, learning, and course correction to reduce the cost and image damage of not meeting internationally agreed-upon goals. Sustainability is a process that tells of a development of all aspects of human life affecting sustenance. It means resolving the conflict between various competing goals, and involves the simultaneous pursuit of economic prosperity, environmental quality, and social equity, famously known as three dimensions or triple bottom line with the resultant vector being technology; hence it is a continually evolving process.

1.3 LIFE CYCLE ANALYSIS

In the beginning there might be a little confusion between life cycle analysis and life cycle assessment, but both evaluate all stages of products or services. Life cycle analysis and life cycle assessment are the same thing, but the latter is the term more widely adopted in the United States, whereas the former is used more often within the United Kingdom. So, what is life cycle analysis (LCA), and what does it tell us? In short, LCA is the act of measuring the environmental impact of a product or service throughout its life cycle, from resource used to create the product or service, across its use by users, to its end of life. An LCA measures the environmental impact of each distinct part involved in creating and using the products and services, such as energy use in the production, fuel use in the transport, and end-of-life ecological costs. This helps us compare products, materials, and method used, providing useful information by which to make decision that could help the environment. There is quite a lot involved in an LCA and it can be quite costly and time-consuming to implement, but it helps us to understand how

Introduction

different products and services, when designed differently, can reduce the impact on our planet.

European agency given definition of both "Life Cycle Analysis" and "Life Cycle Assessment" involves the evolution of the environmental aspects of a product system through all stages of life cycle. Sometimes also called "life cycle approach," "cradle to grave analysis," or "eco-balance," LCA represents a rapidly emerging family of tools and techniques designed to help in environmental management and longer term in sustainable development. The concept of conducting a detailed examination of the life cycle of a product or process is a recent one that emerged in response to increased environmental awareness on the part of the public, industry, and governments.

The immediate precursor of life cycle analysis and life cycle assessments were the global modeling studies and energy audits of the late 1960s and early 1970s. These attempted to assess the resource cost and environmental implications of different patterns of human approaches. LCAs were an obvious extension and became vital to support the development of eco-leveling schemes that are operating or planned in several countries around the world. In order for eco-levels to be granted to choose products, the awarding authority needs to be able to evaluate the manufacturing processes involved, the energy consumption in manufacture and use, and the amount and type of waste generated. To accurately assess the burdens placed on the environment by the manufacturer of an item, one must follow a certain procedure involving two main stages. The first stage is collection of data, and the second is interpretation of that data.

Several different terms have been coined to describe the processes. One of the first terms used was life cycle analysis, but more recently two terms have come to largely replace that one: life cycle assessment (LCA) and life cycle inventory (LCI). These better reflect the different stages of the process. LCA is a potentially powerful tool that can assist regulators to formulate environmental legislation, help manufacturers analyze their processes and improve their products, and perhaps enable consumers to make more informed choices. Like most tools, it must be correctly used. However, a tendency for LCA to be used to "prove" the superiority of one product over another has brought the concept into disrepute in some areas. Taking as an example the case of a manufactured product, LCA involves making detailed measurements during the manufacture of the product, from the mining of the raw materials used in its production and distribution, to its use, possible reuse or recycling, and its eventual disposal. LCAs enable a manufacturer to quantify how much energy and raw materials are used, and how much solid, liquid, and gaseous waste is generated, at each stage of the product's life.

Such a study would normally ignore second-generation impacts, such as energy required to fire the bricks used to build the kilns used for manufacture of raw material. However, deciding which is the "cradle" and which the "grave" for such studies has been one of the points of contention in the relatively new science of LCA, and in order for LCAs to have value there must be standardization of methodology and consensus as to where to set the limits. Much of the focus worldwide to date has been on agreeing on the methods and boundaries to be used when

6   Life Cycle Assessment

making such analysis, and now they are accepted widely. While carrying out an LCA is a lengthy and very detailed exercise, the data collection stage is in theory at least relatively uncomplicated, provided the boundary of the study has been clearly defined, the methodology is rigorously applied, and reliable high-quality data is available. While such a record is helpful and informative, on its own it is not sufficient. Having first compiled the detailed inventory, the next stage should be to evaluate the findings. The second stage of LCA is more difficult, since it requires the interpretation of data and value judgments. An LCI will reveal, for example, how many kilos of pulp, how much electricity, and how many gallons of water are involved in producing a quantity of paper. Only by then assessing these statistics can a conclusion be reached about the product's overall environmental impact. This includes the necessity to make judgments based on assembled figures to assess the likely significance of the various impacts, reported by the World Resources Institute (WRI).

Many problems arise from making decisions without a scientific basis, such as whether three tonnes of emitted sulfur is more harmful than the emission of just a few kilograms of more toxic pollutants, which is necessarily subjective. How can one compare heavy energy demand with heavy water use that imposes greater environmental burdens? How should the use of non-renewable mineral resources like oil gas or coal be compared with the production of pulp for paper manufacturing? How should the combined impact of the landfilling waste, air and groundwater pollution, transport impacts, and so forth be compared with those produced by burning waste from energy production, which contribute emissions predominantly to the air? Some studies attempt to aggregate the various impacts into clearly defined categories, for example the possible impact on the ozone layer, or the contribution to acid rain. Others go still further and try to add aggregated figures to arrive at a single "score" of the product or process being evaluated. It is doubtful whether such simplification will be generally beneficial. Reliable methods for aggregating figures generated by LCA and using them to compare the life cycle impacts of different products do not yet exist. However, a great deal of work is currently being conducted on this aspect of LCA as to arrive at a standardized method of interpreting the collected data. Many times, LCAs have reached different and sometimes contradictory conclusions about similar products. Comparisons are rarely easy because of different assumptions and cutoff points are used, for example, in the case of food packaging, regarding size and form of containers, the performance and production and distribution systems, and the form and type of energy used. To compare two items that are identically in size and distributed and recycled at the same rate is relatively simple, but even they require assumptions. For example, they must consider whether deliveries were made in a nine-tonne truck or a larger one, whether it used diesel or petrol, and drove on congested city center roads, where fuel efficiencies are lower, or on village roads or state/national highways, where fuel efficiency might be better. Recycling introduces a further challenge. In the case of materials like steel and aluminum, which can technically be recycled an indefinite number of times with some melt losses, there is no longer a grave. But in the case of paper, which can

Introduction

theoretically be reprocessed four to five times before fibers are too short or to have viable strength, should calculations assume that it will be recycled four times or not? What return rates, for example, should be assumed for factory refillable containers? For both refillable containers and materials sent for recycling, the transport distance in each specific case is a major influence on the environmental impacts associated with the process. An LCA that concludes that recycling of low-value renewable material in one city is environmentally preferable may not hold for different, more remote cities where reprocessing facilities incur large transport impacts. LCA has begun to be used to evaluate a city or region's future waste management options. The LCA or environmental assessment covers the environmental and resource impacts of alternate disposal processes, as well as those other processes that are affected by disposable strategy such as different types of collection schemes for recyclable material changed transport patterns and so on. The complexity of the task and the number of assumptions that must be made should be accounted for in the calculation of impact.

The concept of life cycle thinking is being practiced globally by adopting LCA. It is rapidly emerging as a decision-making driver for industries, stakeholders, and the government—the decision maker. Many companies around the globe are reexamining their business operation and relationship in fundamental ways. They are exploring the concept of sustainable development, seeking to integrate their pursuit of profitable growth with the assurance of environmental protection and quality of life for present and future generations. LCA attempts to provide a systematic approach to quantifying resource consumption in terms of materials and both thermal and electrical energy, its impact on local, regional, and global environments to air, water, and land associated throughout the life cycle to avoid a piecemeal approach to the system of products, processes, and services.

Major advantages of the life cycle approach include sifting of the environmental pollution problems from various stages, geographic locations, and environmental media, which ensures transparency with better alternate paths available for the mitigation of various pollutants. Hence, LCA is an effective scientific analytical tool for systematic evaluation, referred to as "cradle-to-grave" or even "cradle-to-cradle." It takes into consideration that all product life cycle stages, starting from extracting, transporting, and processing raw materials, manufacturing and product transportation and distribution, use/reuse, and recycling and also waste management, can be optimized to minimize environmental and economic impacts. It is used to measure and compare the environmental impacts of products and services, frequently using computer modeling software.

Most LCA measurements are made by summing the unit of energy consumed in the extraction of raw materials, transport, manufacture, product distribution, and final disposal of a product or service. According to the ISO 14040 series standards, LCA assesses the potential environmental aspects associated with a product or service in four stages:

- Setting a goal and scope of the LCA study.
- Compiling an inventory of relevant inputs and outputs.

8   Life Cycle Assessment

- Evaluating the potential and environmental impacts—local, regional, and global with relevant functional units.
- Interpreting the result of the inventory and impact phase in relation to the objective of the study.

LCA has some limitations. For example, a great deal of basic research must be completed to establish baselines for specific areas and times against which to compare environmental impacts. Also, impacts will vary by type of raw materials, source of power, water, region, and so forth, so it is exceedingly difficult to compare products or processes on a global scale. The business world demands sustainability in any market driven by aspiration of various environmental management tools and their realignments in groups to achieve long-term global goals and targets.

Now companies are eager to adapt different tools to increase competitiveness and achieve sustainable results. Sustainable development can be attainable by LCA through better governance of natural resources, more use of renewable energy, and using BAT and best practices to approach zero emissions, over and above other three pillars of economy, environment, and society.

This book envisages the possibility of integrating LCA, LCC, SLCA, and newly emerging EMS tools to generate results that are more relevant in the pursuit of global goals. Global strategies are developed to promote LCT based on lessons learned from environmental LCA. It will be better to get the whole picture of sustainability, hence it is vital to extend LCA to encompass the organizational along with the environmental, economic, and social. Combining ELCA, SLCA, and OLCA will contribute to an assessment of products, processes, or services that provides more relevant results in the context of sustainability. The only solution lies in the radical quick shift in our thinking about global organizations, that in many countries collaborations should involve policy makers and governmental organizations, especially for developing and emerging economies.

2 Environmental Management System

2.1 BACKGROUND

Since the industrial revolution, scientists universally agree that rapid industrialization and the fast growth of the human population and their activities have harmed the global environment. But it has been multiplied manyfold due to the increasing consumption rate of natural resources because of prevailing modern urban and luxurious lifestyles.

Environmental groups, NGOs, and other public institutions emphasize the necessity of business sustainability to achieve a global economy that supports today's population of 7.6 billion and to meet the needs of the projected 9 billion people in 2050. By mid-century, the mean annual temperature is projected to increase by 1.1°C to 2.3°C under the moderate climate-change scenario of the Intergovernmental Panel on Climate Change, with anticipated deterioration of climatic conditions. Economic development essentially takes place on natural resource bases, which are inestimable. Nothing is infinite; hence depreciation of natural capital is inevitable given human economic activity.

2.2 GLOBAL MOVEMENT

The growing impact of human activities on the planet causes various environmental disasters. It is said that "one cannot manage what one cannot measure," but it is an incredibly challenging task to create single metric that can capture all human impacts on the environment. Global trends towards sustainability to maintain the ecosystem are aroused due to overpopulation, consumption, and simultaneous declines in resource availability. The challenge of sustainable development arises from two major converging trends. Efforts are being through various environmental tools but they do not encompass all the impact parameters. The environment and energy are two sides of the same coin.

Emerging technologies can eliminate or reduce environmental pollution, energy consumption, and intensification of resource exhaustion by alternative materials. These are the major issues dealt with by various government and international organizations who have already been rethinking the role of enterprise in remedial measures. As an important component of society, enterprise has caused numerous problems due to extracting material resources from the Earth. Manufacturing units are not only operating in the pursuit of profit but also undertake social and environmental responsibility by adapting innovative ideas with emerging technologies. They encourage R&D activities with the cooperation

DOI: 10.1201/9781003206750-2

of educational institutes and the help of government, community, customer, and employee stakeholders and by paying attention to the safety of their products and processes with respect to the environment.

The awareness of environmental issues among the public is rapidly spreading around the globe due to the impact of climate change and other natural disasters. The public has the right to know about the social and environmental responsibility performance of companies, and the government is strengthening relevant regulations. Figure 2.1 depicts the global trend of environmental demand for sustainability.

In view of this, an environmental management system becomes crucial. Such a system has grown up over a period of six decades. It comprises all the inputs of natural resources and its mitigation by various environmental tools are required to integrate to implement for all human activities like all manufacturing processes, products, services, transportation, construction, and so forth. The circular economy (CE) is the newest buzzword in sustainable development, emphasizing the conservation of resources through recycling, reuse, replacement, and minimizing adverse environmental impacts, promising economic growth without destruction or waste, and aimed at eliminating waste and the continual use of resources.

Hence, CE is a systemic approach to economic development designed to benefit businesses, society, and the environment, and it aims to gradually decouple growth from the consumption of finite resources. In the CE approach, it is vital to focus on

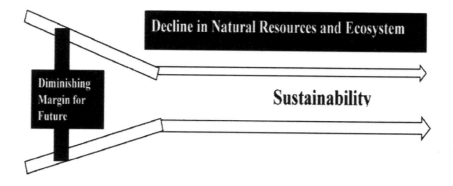

FIGURE 2.1 Global trend of environmental demand for sustainability.

Environmental Management System

renewable and clean sources of energy such as solar and wind. Use of waste materials or by products from other industries by synergizing of multiple industries could transmit benefits to improve the environment, and the security of the supply of raw materials and saving of natural resources increases competitiveness and boosts economic growth.

2.3 NECESSITY OF ENVIRONMENTAL MANAGEMENT SYSTEM

Environmental management is entirely an emerging and dynamic concept. Environmental management is concerned with the management for environment encompassing a business or activity. EMS is the systematic attempt by organizations to identify, measure, document, and reduce their environmental footprint by integrating various functions with the day-to-day affairs of management and decision-making. Industrial growth could stand firmly if the health of the population and industrial workers and their family members are positively addressed.

Environmental tragedies, such as the leakage of MIC gas in the Union Carbide plant in Bhopal, are happening throughout the world regularly. So, it is highly necessary to manage and control environmental deterioration. With the growth of populations and industrialization the problems of overexploitation and natural resources depletion have reached alarming proportions in all parts of the globe, particularly in emerging and developing countries. Pollution of air space, land areas, and bodies of water, including oceans, are taking place rapidly throughout the world. Plastic pollution in the ocean bed is at an alarming stage. To ensure a healthy environment for the present as well as future generations, we need to manage all the components of the environment, adopting all available tools and regulating all industrial processes and products. The presence of EMS may indicate environmental friendliness of an organization, but the uncertainty of measurement related to indicators and indices may yield an unreliable picture of the environmental performance of the organization.

EMS represents the organizational structure, responsibilities, sequences, processes, and preconditions for the implementation of an environmental corporate policy. The basic functions of good environmental management are goal setting; information management; support of decision-making, organizing and planning of environmental management, environmental management programs, piloting, implementation and control, communication, internal and external auditing, and so forth. To control and properly manage pollutants, various governments have developed environmental regulations that organizations must comply with or face penalties, fines, and liability. Facilities often respond to these regulations and problems with successful solutions designed to meet the latest regulations but rarely coordinate their environmental activities into an overall management system. Environmental issues are becoming more complex, and the cost of waste management continues to rise.

The traditional way of addressing environmental issues in a reactive, ad hoc, end-of-pipe manner has proven to be highly inefficient. Increasingly, businesses have realized that environmental problems would be better managed in a systematic way. Just as businesses develop fiscal management systems to promote the efficient use and management of monetary resources, they realize that environmental management systems developed and integrated into the organizational structure will reduce risks from pollution and will help provide an opportunity to be more efficient and organized. EMSs help integrate environmental issues into business decisions and practices. They provide a framework for managing environmental responsibilities in a more systematic way. An EMS approach incorporates periodic review by top management and emphasizes continuous improvement instead of crisis management.

The systematic nature of the EMS allows an organization to focus on implementation and to take a more inclusive and proactive approach. Pollution can be minimized if all the industries and various organizations meticulously implement the EMS. There are many environmental parameters measured by various environmental tools to support five concepts to achieve the goal for sustainable development. In fact, the importance of the environment and its impact has been felt since the 1970s; over the last five decades many tools and instruments have been developed to mitigate the environmental degradation to a reasonable extent. Figure 2.2 shows how the evolution of EMS has taken place to deal with environment, and Figure 2.3 depicts how various input data required from different tools for five different environmental concepts of EMS contribute towards achieving the goal of sustainable development. At present, LCT plays the very vital role of dealing with all input and output analyses of environmental data by adopting LCA. The LCA study needs to generate environmental data through measuring, monitoring, analyzing, and reviewing to identify hot spots and impacts of products, processes, or services.

In view of the large number of environmental parameters, a system was developed to manage it—a methodology developed by the international community as Environmental Management System (EMS) to use it for industries, organizations, and institutions as ISO 14000 series covering various usages. The EMS approach and content described herein are based upon well-established overall approaches as well as detailed advantages. An EMS provides the structure to establish a component of other strategic and business planning efforts for broad environmental performance goals, objectives, and targets and to assess organizational performance in meeting these goals.

An EMS is part of an organization's management system used to develop and implement its environmental policy and manage its environmental aspects. It comprises a set of management processes and procedures that allows an organization to analyses, control, and reduce the environmental impact of its activities, products, and services, and operate with greater efficiency and control. An EMS is appropriate for all kinds of organizations of varying sizes in both the public and private sectors. For an EMS to be effective, it should be involved in the monitoring, tracking, summarizing, and reporting of environmental information to internal and external stakeholders.

There is also a need for integrating cross-functional activities to include environmental training of personnel. Finally, there is the need for formal procedures

Environmental Management System

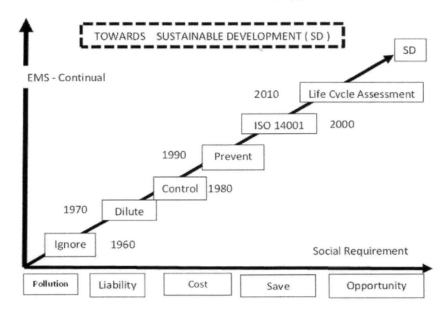

FIGURE 2.2 Evolution of EMS over six decades.

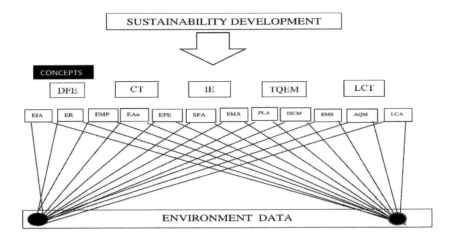

FIGURE 2.3 Various input data required from tools for environmental concepts.

and the availability of these specialized procedures and information to be available to people in new product development, recycling, and pollution prevention. A firm's commitment to an EMS will be a determining factor in the success of the system and the extent of the benefits derived from environmental initiatives. A vigorous debate is now occurring around the question of whether initiatives to improve the environmental performance of corporations, either compliance-driven

14 Life Cycle Assessment

or voluntary, have consistent impacts on the financial performance of these firms. EMS reporting is useful both for internal and external parties depending upon the type of environmental tools used. Whereas LCA, one of the EMS tools can be used both internal as well as external purpose.

2.4 INTERNATIONAL STANDARDS

ISO 14000 refers to a family of voluntary standards and guidance documents to help organizations address environmental issues. Included in the family are standards for EMS, environmental and EMS auditing, environmental labeling, performance evaluation, LCA. In September 1996, the ISO published the first edition of ISO 14001, the specific standard for EMSs. This international voluntary standard is a specification of what is required for an EMS to receive certification or registration under ISO and can be used to guide development of an EMS whether certification is anticipated or not. A second edition of ISO 14001 was published in 2004, updating the standard. Other standards in the series are guidelines, many to help achieve to ISO 14001, although they can be used "standalone." These include the following:

- ISO 14001–1996, 2004, and 2016 EMS.
- ISO 14004–2016 provides guidance and implementation of EMSs.
- ISO 14040–1997 and 2006 Environmental Management—Life Cycle Assessment—Principles and Framework.
- ISO 14041–1998 Environmental Management—Life Cycle Assessment—goal and scope definition and inventory analysis (withdrawn).
- ISO 14042–2000 Environmental Management—Life Cycle Assessment—Life Cycle Impact Assessment (withdrawn).
- ISO 14043–2000 Environmental Management—Life Cycle Assessment—Life Cycle Interpretation (withdrawn).
- ISO 14044–2006 Environmental Management—Life Cycle Assessment—requirements and guidelines.

2.5 IMPLEMENTATION

An EMS enables an organization to establish an environmental policy appropriate to itself; identify the environmental aspects arising from the organization's past, existing, or planned activities, products, or services, to determine those aspects that can have significant impacts on the environment; identify the relevant legislative and regulatory requirements; identify priorities and set appropriate environmental objectives and targets; establish a structure and program to implement the policy and achieve objectives and targets; facilitate planning, control, monitoring, corrective action, auditing, and review activities to ensure both that the policy is complied with and that the environmental management system remains appropriate; and be capable of adapting to changing circumstances. One may find that an

Environmental Management System 15

EMS does not involve a drastic change from the way an organization is conducting business now. In fact, most organizations find that they have many of the pieces of an EMS already in place. The EMS builds on what you are doing well now and provides a structured approach to improve what you want to do better.

2.6 EXTENSION

Sustainable development in its broadest sense includes developing the potential uses of the environment while also making humans able to manage its health: a humane consideration. It strikes a balance between short-term interests and long-term benefits, between economic growth and protection of the environment. As a new paradigm of development environmental sustainability, this indicates effective use of the environment and empowerment of people to design and participate in the process of its management. Hence, it needs a thorough analysis of the strengths, weaknesses, threats, and opportunities for economic development now and in the future. This will create the much-needed awareness for prioritization of economic activities in the country to make the best use of limited available natural resources. Scientists, engineers, and LCA practitioners who develop decision support, or make decisions where sustainability is a concern, should understand the need to view the solutions in terms of LCT and to consider trade-offs between environmental impacts and between the three sustainability dimensions. Designers and engineers who develop products and technical systems should be able to critically read and evaluate LCA information about the alternatives that they are considering, and the environmental sustainability specialists among them should also be able to perform LCA studies to identify hot spots in the system. The applications of LCA and LCT by policy makers and decision makers in government and industry is a key factor for dealing with sustainability.

2.7 REBOOTING

As highlighted in the UN Secretary-General's Earth Day message, countries' responses to the economic crisis should include investment in green jobs and green transition through more resilient infrastructure, including water, energy, transportation, health, and sanitation networks. Low-carbon investments in transportation and energy can deliver more jobs per dollar spent than fossil fuels; seizing these investments can accelerate the transition.

2.8 REDUCTION OF CARBON AND WATER FOOTPRINTS

Countries should avoid bailing out polluting industries unless they commit to becoming carbon neutral and ending fossil fuel subsidies. Climate risk should be part of any financial and policy decisions, and countries should consider putting a price on carbon. International cooperation will be critical to make all of this happen while leaving no one behind.

2.9 REORIENTATION

Countries should explore ways to prepare more ambitious environmental plans and national adaptation processes. Their efforts to reinvigorate the economy following the COVID-19 health crisis should be mutually reinforcing with sustainable development goals (SDGs). During this period, most of the world breathed fresh air and human activities came to a grinding halt for a couple of months, making nature and its wild inhabitants smile for a moment. All of us should reorient our working activities while ready to adopt some innovative and radical way of doing office work or business, keeping long time interest of our earth's nature.

2.10 FACTORS TO CONSIDER

Unfortunately, it has taken the present global pandemic to make everybody to rethink their activities, including how to adopt various environmental management tools. The COVID-19 pandemic has triggered organizational and technological changes to the way businesses to operate. These could adversely affect productivity growth if they erode capital or disrupt the accumulation of physical or human capital. Appropriate policies and regulations concerning finance, construction, and environmental protection can help reduce the frequency of adverse shocks. The present state of economic development, including the state of the environment, makes it necessary to broaden management's understanding of the natural environment. It has been observed throughout the globe that during the period of "Lock Down" and "Shut Down," the pollution levels of both water bodies and atmospheric air have drastically reduced due to closures of industrial activities and a pause in human travel by road, rail, and air. During this period, we have observed the precarious condition of both the haves and have-nots. Some luxury habits need to be restricted to minimize environmental impacts. Now environment regulator is taking help of satellite imagery technology to assess the emission level of not only individual industry but also local and regional pollutants' status of the area. Hence, it has become imperative to consider ecological consequences while setting up brownfield or greenfield projects. Technology is available today to reduce environmental pollution, and it must be used to correct the excesses of ecological brutality and to minimize the degree of environmental degradation. Take, for example, working from home. It may not be the end of the office, but it is the end of the old way of viewing the office and its management. These are important steps forward, but we need an even greater response. There are a few ways national governments and others can continue the momentum this year and better advance the EMS agenda.

2.11 SUSTAINABLE FUTURE

A consensus on ways to recover better and greener, as recently suggested by environmental experts, can provide an important opportunity to foster cooperation and learning between countries. The COVID-19 pandemic has shown us the importance of healthy, connected, and resilient societies. We cannot achieve

Environmental Management System 17

these goals over the long term without collective climate action. Key climate events may be delayed, but the climate emergency cannot. As UN Secretary-General António Guterres said at the Petersburg Climate Dialogue, "they say it's darkest just before the dawn." These are dark days, but they are not days without hope. We have a short and rare opportunity to change our world for the better. We must use the experience of COVID-19 as an impetus to speed up our efforts to secure a safe and sustainable future for all. International cooperation and multilateralism will remain more important than ever. It is time to reinvent and reenergize the way we cooperate and reach decisions, interdependently with a renewed sense of solidarity and urgency among developing and developed nations of the world.

In the present digital era, scientists and technocrats are expected to be globally competent, which means they should have the ability to work efficiently and comfortably in a transnational scientific world with knowledge of environmental impacts on global society. Most of the corporations around the world are revisiting on a continuous basis their business activities, operations, and relationships in a fundamental way in aligning with global environmental and social requirements under the SDGs. They are also exploring the concept of sustainable development, seeking to integrate their pursuit of profitable growth with the assurance of environmental protection and quality of life for present and future generations. Based on this new perspective, some companies are beginning to make significant changes in their policies, commitments, and business strategies. As an example, the real estate and construction sectors can be exceptional to the fact that they are the fat consumer of most of the natural resources including energy and water, if it is analyzed through out of its life. Hence LCA study of the construction industry has been discussed in a subsequent chapter of this book that examines the effort one of the major construction companies to explore how commercial buildings can evolve over time to better meet the need for global sustainable development while enhancing their value to all stakeholders. Contemporary society has undergone a paradigm shift from environmental protection towards sustainability. Sustainability does not only focus on environmental impact; it consists of three dimensions, including the environment, economy, and social well-being, which it seeks to balance and even optimize. Today, sustainability is accepted by all stakeholders as a guiding principle for both for corporate strategies and public policy making. However, the biggest challenge for most organizations remains in the real parameters to measure and control to adopt the sustainability concept and implementing it.

2.12 CONTINUAL IMPROVEMENT

An EMS is a structured system or management tool that, once implemented, helps an organization identify the environmental impacts resulting from its business activities and to improve its environmental performance. The system aims to provide a methodical approach to planning, implementing, and reviewing an organization's environmental management. Most organizations will have systems for managing their human resources, business objectives, and finances as well as occupational health, safety, and security. An EMS will work more effectively if it is designed to operate in line with an organization's existing systems and processes, such as the planning cycle, the setting of targets and improvement programs, corrective and preventive action, and management review. The environmental aspects of an organization are those activities, products, and services of an organization that have or can have an impact on the environment. An EMS enables an organization to identify its environmental aspects and determines which of them can have a significant impact on the environment. This helps an organization understand how it interacts with the environment. This in turn guides an organization in determining where environmental controls or improvements are needed, and in the setting of priorities for action to improve environmental performance. It is heartening to note that industry is responding to the governmental guidelines on the environment. The list of drivers are laws and regulations, technological developments, expansion of global markets, loss of market share or key clients, emerging market opportunities, new employment patterns, new organizational structures, global environmental issues, need to reduce cost, new competitors, potential to improve the bottom line through increased efficiencies, demonstrating leadership and improving image and reputation, compliance and risk management, personal passion, and commitment to making a difference. Environmental indicators tend to relate to the environmental sphere closest to human activity and can include economic, social, and sustainability parameters too. They measure the quality of the living and working environment, usually for the three spheres of air, land, and water, and may include measures for productive use of resources. Ecological indicators relate more to ecosystems. Because it is holistic, systemic, and rigorous, environmental LCA is the preferred technique when it comes to compiling and assessing information about potential environmental impacts of a product. It has been standardized in the ISO 14040 and 14044 and is applied by practitioners globally. As emerging techniques, SLCA and OLCA are likely to play key roles in complementing ELCA-related inputs.

3 Life Cycle Assessment

3.1 BACKDROP

Organizations all over the world are now in search of excellence in their energy and environmental achievements. It is well known that the main source of environmental deterioration and energy consumption and reduction of all emissions needs innovative technology to adopt to bring down pollution level, if possible, to zero. Now in some of leading industries, their emissions are not any more confinement to the point sources and process related because of emerging and advanced technologies. They also use IT technologies like artificial intelligence (AI), cloud, and blockchain adopted for manufacturing of the products and handling over all transportation system and the supply chain. The challenge of future decades is to help to reduce climate change through clean sustainable technology. There are various approaches to environmental management for sustainable development. Numbers of ideas and methods supporting better management have arisen within several disciplines. Since environmental awareness has increased in society, more attention has been focused on various environmental management concepts and tools to achieve the goal for a sustainable future.

Achieving sustainable development depends broadly on five concepts, including LCT, DFE, CT, IE, and TQEM, of course with the support of AI and other IT-driven support. However, there are a number of methodologies to achieve the goal, which can be broadly divided into two broad categories covering the ecosphere and technosphere and are more than one and half dozen various tools to deal with environmental management. Those common around the globe are LCA, LCC, environmental risk assessment (ERA), environmental impact assessment (EIA), environmental management planning (EMP), environmental auditing (EA), cost benefit analysis (CBA), Health Risk Analysis (HRA), and so forth.

In the early years of LCA history, environmental concerns were addressed inconsistently by various methods. Only the organization's interests in terms financial benefits were taken into account, and environmental issues were neglected in LCA studies carried out during that time. But energy and environment are two sides of the same coin. If one can save energy, one will save the environment. LCA's origins date back six decades to energy analysis studies in the 1960s and 1970s. The LCA of packaging studies by Coca-Cola's confinement to limited objective could not be appreciated probably due to partial interpretation. But since then, LCA has improved to a great extent and various environmental impacts have widened and sharpened.

LCA grew into a broad tool for exploring potential impacts in terms of several environmental metrics and resource depletion in the early 1990s under the auspices of leading global industry leaders, educational institutes both individually as well as in conjunction with organizations like the UNEP, USEPA, SETAC, IVL,

DOI: 10.1201/9781003206750-3

19

20 Life Cycle Assessment

EU, Chalmers University, and Leiden University, who helped develop international standards with the help of the ISO. In the last two decades, developments in the methodology of LCA have been connected to the understanding of LCA as an instrument for decision-making. Now LCA has been established as a prospective assessment of the consequences of a choice between several substitutable product or decision-making context in terms of the stakeholders involved, issues that are important for sustainability of the relevant product or process system. As inventories got more complex, the initial focus on accounting for the physical flows in a product life cycle was gradually extended with a translation of the inventory results into environmental impact potentials. In other words, from a list of resource uses and emissions a set of indicator scores for an assessed product was calculated, representing contributions to several impact categories, such as climate change, acidification, eutrophication, resource scarcity, and human toxicity. A detailed chronological development of the LCA movement is given in Table 3.1.

TABLE 3.1
Chronological Development of Life Cycle Assessment

Year	LCA: Chronological Development	Remarks
1963	First LCA: Energy Oriented Study	World Energy Conference
1969	First LCA: Comparing Beverage Containers	Coca-Cola Industry
1970	Input–Output Analysis for Environment (EIO-LCA Method)	Wassily Leontief, Carnegie Mellon University (CMU)
1974	First Peer Reviewed LCA Study: Nine Beverage Container Alternatives	USA EPA
1984	First Impact Assessment Method Based on Critical Volumes Introduced	BUS
1989	Commercial LCA Software GaBi First Version	PE International, Germany (Now Think Step)
1990	First Version of SimaPro LCA Software	Pre-Consultants, the Netherlands
1990	First Workshop on Framework of LCA	SETAC, USA
1992	Impact Assessment Methodology CML-92	Heijungs et al.
1993	LCA Framework, Terminology and Methodology Developed	SETAC, USA
1996	First Issue of *International Journal of Life Cycle Assessment* Published	IJLCA
1997	First International Standard on LCA Principles and Framework	ISO 14040
1998	Standard on LCA Goal and Scope Definition	ISO 14041
1999	Damage Oriented Methodology Eco-Indicator 99 Emerges	Goedkoop and Spriensma
2000	Standard on Life Cycle Impact Assessment	ISO 14042

Life Cycle Assessment

TABLE 3.1 *(Continued)*

Year	LCA: Chronological Development	Remarks
2000	Standard on Life Cycle Impact Interpretation	ISO 14043
2002	Life Cycle Initiative Released	UNEP/SETAC
2003	The LCI Database Eco Invent Version 1.0	Eco invent
2006	Establishing of a General Methodological Framework and Guideline for LCA	ISO 14040 and ISO 14044
2008	A Framework for Life Cycle Sustainability Analysis Proposed	Klopffer
2009	Guidelines for Social LCA of Products	UNEP/SETAC and Life Cycle Initiative
2010	International Reference Life Cycle Data System (ILCD) Handbook	(JRC, EC) European Union
2011	Global Guidance Principles for LCA Databases	UNEP/SETAC and Life Cycle Initiative
2012	Product Environmental Footprint and Organizational Environmental Footprint	European Commission
2013	Guidance on Organizational LCA	UNEP/SETAC and Life Cycle Initiative
2016	Attributional and Consequential LCA in ILCD	IJLCA

3.2 FRAMEWORK

The concept of LCT is being practiced by using the environmental management tool popularly known as LCA, which has become useful and prevalent in research, industry, and policy making. It has evolved rapidly from a product attributional tool to one that is being more commonly used by policy makers and standards bodies for broad and interrelated effects beyond the product, for example, to help design large-scale consequential environmental and energy solutions. Enabling complex issues to be assessed over a life cycle basis is beneficial in many respects. Table 3.2 provides advantages of LCT, when adopted in LCA studies encompassing all phases from "cradle to grave." However, benefits are not obtained if procedures are not properly followed.

In principle, LCA is simply a scientific approach to embrace all activities that go into making, transporting, using, and disposing of a product or service. LCA avoids shifting of the environmental pollution burdens from various stages, geographic locations, and environmental media, which ensures better alternate paths available for the mitigation of various pollutants. Hence, LCA is an effective analytical tool for the systematic evaluation of various environmental impacts,

TABLE 3.2

Life Cycle Thinking When Adopted in LCA Studies

SL. No.	Departments	Steps Taken for Improvement	Gaps in Benefits
1	Design	All phases integrated, which contributes total impact	When single phase segregated reflects partial impacts
2	Plant	Hot spots identified for performance improvement	Environmental problem can be fixed or may escape unnoticed
3	Supply Chain	Capable of covering whole supply chain system	Shifting of problems may take place if not wholly covered
4	Marketing	Evaluation and advantage shown in the entire system	Unable to compare in totality
5	Consumers	Get information on environmental impacts of all phases	Should provide all information, if not covered all phases
6	Local Market	Attracts local consumers based on environmentally friendly image	Short-term decision may lead to environmental disadvantages
7	Image Building	Financial investors look for better environmental image for further investment to support sustainable project	Environmental impacts create poor performance and leads to inefficiencies in overall management system due to not being cost effective

either of a product or service system, from extraction and processing of raw materials through manufacture, delivery, use, and finally, its waste management. The functional unit is the second basic term in an LCA. It has an especially significant role to play in terms of inventory and impact analysis. For example, for the cement industry, the functional unit is the kg/tonne of production. It is important to note that systems with equivalent functions are compared. Therefore, it is possible to define services as systems and compare them with tangible products based on equivalent functions by means of the functional units. This requires rigorous data collection with interpretation and review, which helps the industry in both internal and external decision-making for its sustainability in the local and global perspectives. It is a powerful tool that can be used to place the product in its role for sustainable development. In recent years, LCA has been watched with keen interest as a method for evaluating environmental load to realize sustainability. Taking as an example the case of manufactured products, Figure 3.1 illustrates the process and boundary of cement manufacturing, along with the extended boundary for cement manufacturing unit. Now most of the cement plants in India have their captive power plants (CPPs). In view of this the boundary has been extended to its CPP. It must be linked for input of electrical energy to the cement plant, depending on the goal and scope of the LCA study. The environmental impacts associated with any process or product must analyze

Life Cycle Assessment

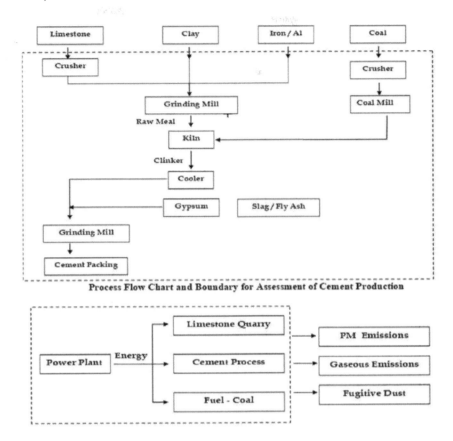

FIGURE 3.1 Extended boundary for life cycle assessment in cement production.

the entire life of that product and consider the environmental impact or burdens of each activity along the way. Thus, product or process LCAs typically consider the extraction of the raw materials and manufacturing processes that turn those raw materials into useful products, transportation of those products, their use, and their eventual disposal or reuse. The scope of study is often called "cradle-to-grave" or, including the reuse potential, "cradle-to-cradle" LCA. If the impact is evaluated up to the product only, it is known as "cradle-to-gate." Figure 3.2 depicts types of LCAs depending on the goal and scope of the studies and inventory, impact assessment, and interpretation for application of alternative paths for continual improvement.

LCA studies become vital to support the development of eco-labeling schemes that are operating or planned in several countries around the world. Quantifying energy and resource flows at each step in the life of a product or process is vital. The emissions from those flows and its impact cover on the complex ecosystem locally, regionally, and globally. To make that impossible task manageable, LCA practitioners integrate primary and secondary data and make

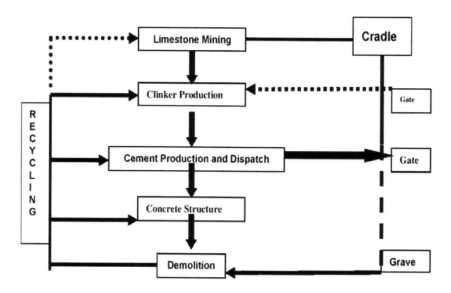

FIGURE 3.2 Life cycle assessment of cement industry.

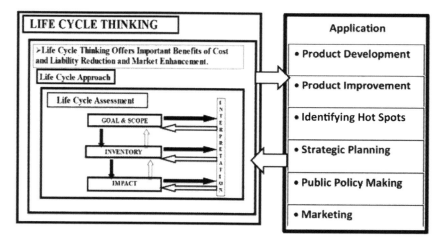

FIGURE 3.3 LCT-LCA stages and application.

some simplifying assumptions at every step of the entire flow and use software that employs computer databases in ways that would not have been feasible a decade ago. Various international organizations are always working on LCA activities consisting of four well-defined and distinct stages in the entire procedure, such as goal and scope definition, inventory analysis, impact assessment, and its interpretation for its application as shown in Figure 3.3. LCA is iterative in nature.

Life Cycle Assessment 25

LCAs enable a manufacturer to quantify how much energy and raw materials are used, and how much solid, liquid, and gaseous waste is generated at each stage of the product's life. Such a study would normally ignore second-generation impacts, such as the energy required to fire the bricks used to build the kilns used to manufacture the raw material. However, deciding which is the "cradle" and which the "grave" for such studies has been one of the points of contention in the relatively new science of LCA, and for LCAs to have value there must be standardization of methodologies and consensus as to where to set the limits. While carrying out an LCA is a lengthy and incredibly detailed exercise, the data collection stage is in theory at least relatively uncomplicated, provided the boundary of the study has been clearly defined, the methodology is rigorously applied, and reliable, high-quality data are collected.

3.3 GOAL AND SCOPE

LCA is an environmental management tool for businesses to achieve sustainable development, which requires the ability to rationalize on the lines of life cycle thinking. In the last decade, there have been many advances in LCA methodology, especially through the scientific work of the Society of Environmental Toxicology and Chemistry (SETAC). The ISO has promoted the standardization of these methods. There has been extensive development and trials by the ISO for bringing uniformity in conducting all four stages of LCA through the publication of ISO standards for the distinct stages of LCA study. In ISO 14040, LCA is defined as "compilation and evaluation of the inputs, outputs and potential environmental impacts of a product/process system throughout its life cycle." ISO standard 14044 states some basic requirements like recording of data and its validation. Besides ensuring accordance with the explicit requirements of the standards, the ISO standards require a review/monitor to ensure that the methods adopted to carry out the life cycle assessment are scientifically and technically valid. For the inventory phase, the most critical issue is the way data is collected and recorded. Impact assessment per ISO guidelines requires that the characterization should be documented in a transparent manner and that selection and definition of the impact categories should be identified and justified as per the goal and scope of the study.

LCA interpretation and understanding of the results will greatly help in decision-making, which would be beneficial both in the planning of environmental strategies and in governing business in the present world. Industry can contribute to society by operating in a more sustainable way and finding a roadmap that consumes less energy and conserves resources judiciously and optimally. Sustainable development is the need of the hour. Achieving sustainability requires LCT among scientists, plant/environmental engineers, and managers of the cement industry as its emissions of carbon dioxide are second only to those of thermal power stations. Production can no longer be performed in isolation and, hence, must consider interactions among various industries to utilize one another's waste for better global and ecological balance. An advantage of the cement industry is having the world's best and biggest incinerators, namely, kilns, to consume all types of hazardous wastes, including those of other industries, which otherwise would have been disposed of by polluting the atmosphere to a greater extent. Implementing LCA studies will only yield tangible benefits to any industry with a serious commitment and sincere efforts by management.

The first important initiation step in carrying out an LCA is defining the goal. It is worthwhile spending the extra time and effort to define clearly the main environmental issues to be tackled. In this initial stage both the subject and the scope of the LCA are defined according to the intended purpose of the study. As the study progresses and more insights are gained, the goal definition can be revised accordingly. Goal and scope can be formulated by giving a general picture of the characteristics of LCA by defining the following few aspects like its scope, purpose, and target group. It is important to identify the level of detail required for the application of the results remembering that the results of this study can never be more accurate than what the input allows. Therefore, efforts should be made to specify the level of detail, for instance over space and time.

The subject to be studied and its specification should clearly describe details relating to the product, its amount, the time span, and its function to quantify total input and output. The purpose of the study may be for internal or external use on products or processes for the planning needed for environmental improvement. LCA entails comparing and quantifying the environmental parameters for various products or processes with distinct set of inputs to prepare a road map for individual requirements. Studies meant for external target groups or agencies usually need more elaboration covering all aspects and more extensive evidence than internal studies to identify the priority of hot spots for minimizing environmental impact. Support in decision-making involves showing results, and improvement analysis provides the information needed for decision-making.

3.4 INVENTORY ANALYSIS

The LCI analysis step involves compilation of an inventory comprising relevant inputs and outputs of a product or process system, covering multiple environmental aspects. The data inventory takes place for each unit process or activity defined in the system. Depending on the study and aims, data may be collected firsthand from measurements and estimates of key activities or may be based on information drawn from existing LCA databases. Distinct levels of consideration are possible, including individual processes and sub-systems (e.g., energy supply, transport). A complete study may consist of several different layers of analysis from specific activities up to the whole life cycle of a product.

The LCI portion of the study is often considered in stages. A cradle-to-gate inventory for cement would include all resources and energy required to produce cement, the "gate" of the plant. A cradle-to-grave inventory would cover all unit processes extending from the original resources on to the final disposal into the environment. Data analysis considers environmental inputs

Life Cycle Assessment

and outputs for an example of LCI data for construction industry. Tools and software are available for assistance. In a fully executed LCA study, all the environmental inputs and outputs associated are considered. LCI has demonstrated considerable benefit as it is an accounting system for encompassing total mass and energy flows. It builds upon conventional process management techniques based on inputs of all raw materials, energy along with construction engineering technology and quality control, but it demands a consistency of accounts across many operations and life cycle activities.

Managers and engineers recognize that LCI can help them keep more accurate and more comprehensive inventories of energy consumption and raw materials usage—and doing so while providing a "zoom lens" from unit process to complete facilities, to corporate divisions, to the level of the company or across the industry and finally the government and policy maker to take appropriate decision for sustainability both for industry as well as overall environment. This process can help identify savings and/or uncover alternative fuels or raw materials or how to encourage further to produce durable concrete structures by the policy maker to achieve improvement in environmental parameters.

Identification of specific data and its collection depends on goal and scope of LCA study. The challenges of data collection need practical guidance on how to collect throughout supply chain for each item. The collection of data is time consuming because quality data is required on many processes and many items in each process, and because the appropriate data is often not readily available. Basic pollutants emitted from different activities need to be measured and analyzed by standard methods. Each box in the flowchart represents a particular process or cluster of processes. For each process or cluster of processes, one needs to collect information on the raw material, thermal and electrical energy input and output flows keeping data on all types of emission covering other environmental aspects. Design a questionnaire/data information sheet; collect the data; and check the gathered data for consistency. It is important to check whether the data are complete and whether they correspond with data from other sources.

One way of checking data is to draw up simple balance sheets for each process, because the total input of a process should equal the total output, including emissions and waste. These balance sheets may be based on the product's mass or on a specific element, such as carbon. Valuable time can be saved by adequate planning, so start collecting data as soon as possible because this takes most of the time. It is one of the toughest and most important tasks in an LCA study and depends on the cooperation of all concerned for detailed compilation of relevant data. It is useful to make estimates before collecting data because this can provide a feeling for the figures involved and may enable you to identify missing data. When designing and formulating questionnaires, one should bear in mind that most of data providers are unfamiliar with LCA and may easily misinterpret the questions. Always remember that the reliability of the result will depend on the quality of the data. Detailed input and output of a cement plant is given in Table 3.3. This

28   Life Cycle Assessment

TABLE 3.3

Material Balance for 1 Tonne of Clinker of 2.75 MTPA Capacity Cement Plant

Inputs	Quantity (kg)	Outputs	Quantity (kg)
Limestone	1496	Clinker	1000
Coal	140.3	CO_2	828.4
Other	15.11	SO_2	Below detectable limits
		Nox	0.86
Air (Kiln)	1114	PM (Kiln)	0.22
Air (Cooler)	1500	Dust in Cooler	0.12
		Exist Air	2435.8
Total Input	4265.4	Total Output	4265.4

Note: This is a typical case for illustrative purposes.

table gives a clear picture of the hot spots to identify and how to take appropriate action to minimize different impacts on continual basis.

3.5 DATA SOURCE

Data can be classified into two groups, namely, primary and secondary sources. The primary sources are from actual determinations of various test samples collected and tested. To get a better view of environmental impact wherever data is not available, data from literature is also included. Prior to the data collection and collation, it is important to record the input and output figures of one year in each unit for impact study. Each data set thus obtained (primary or secondary) focuses on the main materials used, their consumption, thermal from coal, electrical, total production, total emissions, and other environmental issues. The geographical locations are recorded in detail to get a balanced representation of the whole specific area. Production and manufacturing processes are intended to be representative of current technology and plants. Thus, the primary and secondary data so collected is the most recent year (say, one-year data, which needs validation for the study) and refer to the current practices being followed at the best plant using the same technology and elsewhere in the country or even world.

3.6 DATA VARIABILITY AND CONSISTENCY

The secondary data collected from the plant is the average of three year's operation time. But validation of plant data was made for one year by taking measurements of major emissions. Since the production is constant, the various inputs and outputs of various sections are nearly constant. Wherever there is variation, it was explained. However, the variations in data on the primary sources are within a reasonable range on a case-to-case basis under certain circumstances.

Life Cycle Assessment 29

3.7 VALIDATION

As LCI data quantity is meaningful only if the inflow and outflow are regulated in relation to a well-defined system, all input and output data were collected as per guidelines of ISO system. The chemical analysis of material inputs and outputs, like emissions and products, are to be carried out for validation. Major emissions are monitored at the plant level for validation. However, some default emission factors are also adopted due to some gaps in the required data.

3.8 PROCESS FLOW

The inventory analysis forms the core of LCA and is the most time-consuming activity. It is split here into four steps: designing the process flowchart, collecting the data, defining the system boundaries, and finally, processing the data. These steps describe the gathering and processing of the environmental interventions that appear during the life cycle of a product or process. This step introduces the first part: constructing the process flowchart. It is recommended that all steps dealing with the inventory analysis be read before work is begun on any one of them because constructing the flowchart is an iterative process that one may have to repeat several times. The process flowchart is a qualitative and graphical representation of all relevant processes involved in the life cycle of the system studied. It is composed of a sequence of processes represented by boxes, linked by material flows represented by arrows. It is recommended that this convention be used consistently. The main goal of the process flowchart is to create an overview; hence, one should focus on the most relevant processes and environmental interventions rather than striving for 100-percent coverage. Depending on goal definition either one needs a comprehensive flowchart with relatively little detail or a limited flowchart which focuses on a few processes in much more detail. Put this in the center of one's process flowchart and identify relevant processing steps along with major material and energy inputs and outputs.

Therefore, extend the process flowchart with the processes which appear before and after the manufacture of the product. The previous stages will include the mining of major manufacturing and processing of raw materials and components. A process flowchart should also indicate where power is generated in the same manufacturing unit. A few boxes can usually be combined into one or two boxes so that they can be more easily handled. You can, for instance, integrate all the transactions of one activity into a single box. You will discover that the complexity of a process flowchart largely depends on the way in which data can be obtained. Keep in mind that one should concentrate on those steps that generate the largest environmental impacts. Early on in an LCA, it may be difficult to identify these steps, but it will become simpler as the study progresses. In this initial stage one should try to obtain a broad view without going into too much detail.

The flowchart is only a model of reality. It could be helpful to arrange flowchart such that it matches the information sources. The outcome of this step is a

30   Life Cycle Assessment

graphical representation of the subject under study. In principle, a process flow-chart should start at the extraction of materials from the environment by a mining step and include any other inputs involved. It should end with the product (cradle-to-gate) or emissions and waste (cradle-to-grave). However, at each step the corresponding emissions and waste generated should be included. After constructing an initial process flowchart, one may start to collect data. During this collection phase, one may discover that some process steps would require to be distributed further because no general information can be obtained. However, one should remember to concentrate on those steps that are suspected of contributing most to the environmental impact.

3.9   FUNCTIONAL UNIT

The functional unit in any LCA study plays a vital role because the functional unit always referred to all inputs and outputs to determine all environmental parameters and its impact (e.g., GWP, AP, HT) for cement industry common functional is considered per tonne of type of product, because cement plants process huge amount of raw materials to produce 8000–10,000 tonnes per day of clinker, with other blending materials and gypsum, it produces more cement. The functional unit is reference point for deciding unique process to include and to what extent they are drawn. It is therefore essential to ensure that functional unit fully captures the relevant functional aspects of the goal of the study system to support a fair and relevant quantitative comparison of alternate ways for providing knowledge of functions provided by the alternate product system must be used to define a functional unit. The functional unit right from the beginning should be well analyzed before finalizing because it is significantly influenced the way LCA performed it is resulting an interpretation specially in comparative studies plays a very crucial role.

3.10   SYSTEM BOUNDARIES

This step deals with the specification of the system boundaries. Having created the process flowchart and begun collecting data, one must now have some insight into the critical processes that must be included and into the availability of data. This insight together with the goal definition, will allow one to define the system boundaries. In the beginning one needs the preliminary results of the three preceding steps: goal definition, process flowchart, and the data collected. One can then determine which parts need lesser or further detail. LCA deals with the environmental impact of a product or process during its entire life cycle. This environmental load comprises all extractions from and all emissions into the environment which arise during the life of the product. LCA should therefore specify extractions and emissions. Many processes generate several distinct products because of co-production, recycling, or waste processing. The result from this step will include a description of how the boundary between the environment and the system studied has been set up and

Life Cycle Assessment 31

which emissions and extractions will be considered; a description of how the boundary with other related systems has been defined in cases of co-production, recycling, and waste processing; the reasons for excluding certain processes; and finally, a list of the processes for which data is lacking and which are expected to have considerable influence. After completion of this step the collection of data can be continued. When the process boundaries are described and sufficient data has been collected, one may continue with the next step of the processing of data.

3.11 ALLOCATION PROCEDURE

One of the most complex components of modeling data for an LCI is correctly allocating input and output quantities to co-products so that all flows are fairly given to each product output.

> Wherever possible, allocation should be avoided by dividing the unit process to be allocated into two or more sub-processes and collecting the input and output data related to these sub-processes or expanding the product system to include the additional functions related to the co-products. Where allocation cannot be avoided, the system inputs and outputs should be partitioned between its various products or functions in a way that reflects the underlying physical relationships between them, i.e., they must reflect the way in which the inputs and outputs are changed by quantitative changes in the products or functions delivered by the system. Where physical relationship alone cannot be established or used as the basis for allocation the inputs should be allocated between the products and functions in a way that reflects other relationships between them. For example, environmental input and output data might be allocated between co-products in proportion to the economic value of the products.

3.12 IMPACT ASSESSMENT

Life Cycle Impact Assessment (LCIA) evaluates the possible environmental impact associated with measured environmental inputs and outputs. It is important to note here that LCA is not a single-issue tool; rather, the analysis encompasses numerous environmental issues (e.g., energy, air pollution, climate change), thus allowing for a broad consideration of the impact of the system. The results of an LCI study will be a quantitative profile of environmental parameters; information may be first examined at a disaggregated level right from the inventory (e.g., carbon dioxide, nitrogen oxide) or may be grouped or aggregated according to environmental indicator categories like greenhouse gases. The selection of impact categories can either align with traditional categories like global warming, acidification and resource depletion or it can define various other categories that represent specific issues for the decision maker in the given procedure. The framework for the procedure should be laid down by the concept of associating the LCI results with the environment. Thus, the issues of concern or what to protect are identified as LCIA categories. Table 3.4 depicts impact categories

TABLE 3.4
Impact Categories

Inventory	Impact Category	Justification
Limestone, Coal, Clay, etc.	Resource Depletion	Elemental analysis of material inputs expressed in kg Sb eq.
CO_2	Global Warming	These GHG are accounted for Global warming
CO	Human Toxicity Global Warming , Ecotoxicity	CO is a human and animal toxicant, as well as impact on Ozone formation and GHG too. It participates in first two of these environmental mechanism without losing its potency,
NOx	Acidification Global Warming	Double counting should be avoided.
SO_2	Acidification Ecotoxicity	SO_2 contributes to deteriorating human health through PM and restricts the visibility.
$PM_{2.5}$	Human Toxicity Ecotoxicity	Suspended particulate matter below $PM_{2.5}$ has great human health hazard.
Heavy Metals	Human Toxicity	These elements participate in the impact category human toxicity.
Organic Pollutants	Human Toxicity	Participate in human health toxicity category,

of several types and properties for classifying inventory. LCA involves making detailed measurements during manufacture of the product, from the mining of the raw material used in this production and the product distribution, through to its use, possible reuse, or recycling and its disposal.

The LCIA is not comprehensive even on a relative basis. Gaps and omissions in inventory data and LCIA methods and results are inevitable due to many factors. The next element of the LCIA framework concerns the assignment of inventory results to various categories. Several basic impact category classes are recognized that user must distinguish and consider in planning and conducting an LCIA. These include parallel mechanisms—the same emissions may contribute to two or more exclusive categories. Hence the emission should be allocated over the relevant categories to avoid double counting, which is a key factor. Table 3.5 shows increases in blended cement production and their impact, and Table 3.6 shows product variation effects on its three major impacts.

Serial mechanisms are where an emission agent may participate in two or more categories one after the other; there is a need to consider if the categories should also be considered depending upon the intensity of the impacts. Indirect mechanisms are where the products of one category (e.g., the original causing

Life Cycle Assessment

TABLE 3.5
Increased Blended Cement Production and Its Impact

Cement Plant	GWP (kg CO$_2$ equiv.)	AP (kg SO$_2$ equiv.)	CO$_2$ (kg)	NOx (kg)	SO$_2$ (kg)	Dust (kg)
Plant A (10% PPC Increase)	1490	1600	825	2.23	0.0351	0.171
Plant A (20% PPC Increase)	1440	1550	799	2.16	0.0341	0.167
Plant B (10% PPC Increase)	1140	1010	723	1.41	0.0281	0.154
Plant B (10% PSC Increase)	1120	995	711	1.38	0.0281	0.153
Plant C (5% PPC Increase)	1020	846	664	1.19	0.0147	0.142
Plant D (10% PPC Increase)	2540	2390	1550	3.36	0.0382	0.165
Plant D (20% PPC Increase)	2460	2310	1500	3.25	0.0374	0.163

TABLE 3.6
Comparison of Product Alternatives

Cement Type	GWP (kg CO$_2$ per tonne)	ED (MJ)	LU (m^2 yr)
OPC	778	3926	0.23
PPC (35% Fly ash)	572	3173	0.17
PSC (50% Slag)	490	2871	0.15
Saving (PPC)	206	753	0.06
Saving (PSC)	288	10 55	0.08

the release of another substance) may be the starting point for another category; there is a need to consider if the other categories should be included. Combined mechanisms are impacts caused by a combination of two or more emissions; one school of thought is that assumptions are made regarding the background concentration of the other emitted substances.

The second step of classification is assigning inventory inputs/outputs to applicable impact categories. Classification depends on whether the inventory item is an input or an output, what the disposition of the output is and in some cases the material properties for a particular inventory item. One inventory item may have multiple properties and therefore would have multiple impacts. For example, CO_2 and NO_x are both responsible for global warming but CO_2 has prominent role for global warming; whereas NO_x has the potential to create acidification also. Output inventory items from a process may have varying dispositions, such as direct release (to air, water, or land), treatment or recycle/reuse. Outputs with direct release dispositions are classified into impact categories for which impacts will be calculated in the characterization phase of the LCIA. Outputs sent to treatment are considered inputs to a treatment process and impacts are not calculated until direct releases from that process occur. Outputs to recycle/reuse are considered inputs to previous processes and impacts are not directly calculated for outputs that go to recycle/reuse. Note that a product is also an output of a process; however, product outputs are not used to calculate any impacts. Once impact categories for each inventory item are classified, life cycle impact category indicators are quantitatively estimated through the characterization step.

3.13 LIMITATIONS AND UNCERTAINTIES

The purpose of an LCIA is to evaluate the relative potential impacts of a product / process system for various impact categories. There is no intent to measure the actual impacts or provide spatial or temporal relationships linking the inventory to specific impacts. The LCIA is intended to provide a screening level evaluation of impacts. In addition to lacking temporal or spatial relationships and providing only relative impacts, LCA is also limited by the availability and quality of the inventory data. Complete data collection can be very time consuming and expensive.

Sometimes, confidentiality issues may also inhibit the availability of primary data. Uncertainties are also inherent in chemical ranking and scoring systems. The scoring of toxicity properties approach used for human health and ecotoxicity effects is a very cumbersome effort. Systems that do not consider the fate and transport of chemicals in the environment can contribute to misclassifications of chemicals with respect to risk. Unless a sizable number of studies on these aspects is available, it may not give an exact scenario because it takes a lot of time to collect data on toxicity either in humans or in the ecosystem. Also, uncertainty is introduced where it was assumed that all chronic endpoints are equivalent, which is likely not the case. However, it should be noted that in the early stages of an LCA study, chemical toxicity is often not considered at all.

This methodology is an attempt to consider chemical toxicity where it is often ignored. Uncertainty in the inventory data depends on the responses to the availability of data and other limitations identified during inventory data collection. These uncertainties are carried into impact assessment. In general, in LCA, there is uncertainty in the inventory data, which includes but is not limited to the following: missing individual inventory items, missing processes or sets of data due to non-measurement, estimation uncertainty needs special attention, and allocation uncertainty/working with aggregated data. The goal definition and scoping

Life Cycle Assessment   35

processes help reduce the uncertainty from missing data, although it is certain that some missing data will still exist. As far as possible, the remaining uncertainties are reduced primarily through quality assurance/control measures to the greatest possible extent.

Many studies are taken to a point where results are expressed as selected environmental indicators or scores, be it for large scale system comparisons, technology scenarios, or internal improvement assessments. LCA provides structure and direction to help decision makers focus on key priorities for environmental sustainability. Sets of indicators have been developed, addressing commonly agreed upon and important environmental impact categories. Note, however, that additional environmental and other analysis will still be necessary to complete any decision. LCA provides structure and direction to help decision makers focus on key priorities for environmental sustainability.

3.14 GREENHOUSE GAS

The "greenhouse effect," is defined as the changes in the Earth's climate caused by a changed heat balance in the Earth's atmosphere. After water vapor, CO_2 is the most important greenhouse gas (GHG). Normally, billions of tonnes of carbon in the form of CO_2 are absorbed by the oceans and vegetation and are emitted to the atmosphere annually through natural processes. When at equilibrium, the changes between absorption and emission are roughly balanced. The additional anthropogenic sources of GHGs present in the atmosphere may have shifted that equilibrium, acting as a "thermal blanket," and trapping heat from reflected sunlight that would otherwise pass through the atmosphere.

Altering the atmosphere by trapping more heat has been modeled to have a wide variety of effects on the earth's climate, including longer growing seasons, droughts, floods, increased glaciations, loss of the polar ice caps, sea level rise and other displacements, including direct effects on human health through biological agents. The speeds of these projected effects, coupled with their widespread nature, imply a devastating effect on the entire biosphere. The Intergovernmental Panel on Climate Change (IPCC) global climate change model is used to estimate the potential impacts to the environment from global warming. This model converts quantities of GHGs into CO_2 equivalents using IPCC-defined global warming potential equivalency factors. Global Warming Potential (GWP) equivalency factors compare the ability of each GHG to trap heat in the atmosphere relative to the heat-trapping ability of CO_2. GHG data obtained for each LCA stage are multiplied by the relevant GWP100 (over a 100-year life span) to produce CO_2 equivalent values. As the equivalency factors are unitless values, any unit of weight can be used if the unit of measurement is stated explicitly and is consistent throughout the calculation.

This process is done for each GHG, with the decisive step being the summation of all CO_2 equivalents. The final sum, known as the Global Warming Index (GWI),

36 Life Cycle Assessment

indicates the product's potential contribution to global warming for each life cycle stage. The following equation is used to calculate the GWI: Global Warming Index = Σi wi x GWPi, where wi = weight of inventory flow i per functional unit of product. GWPi = Global Warming Potential equivalency factor evaluated at 100 years = weight of CO_2 with the same heat-trapping potential as a gram of inventory flow. A 100-year life span was selected as the most suitable for the goal of this effort, although other bases for calculating potential equivalency are also available.

3.15 ACIDIFICATION POTENTIAL

Acidification, or acid rain, as it is commonly known, occurs when emissions of sulfur dioxide (SO_2) and oxides of nitrogen (NO_x) react in the atmosphere with water, oxygen, and oxidants to form various acidic compounds. This mixture forms a mild solution of sulfuric acid and nitric acid. Sunlight increases the rate of most of these reactions. These compounds then fall to the earth in either wet form (such as rain, snow, and fog) or dry form (such as gas and particles). About half of the acidity in the atmosphere falls back to earth through dry deposition as gases and dry particles. The wind blows these acidic particles and gases onto buildings, and trees. In some instances, these gases and particles can eat away the things on which they settle. Dry deposited gases and particles are sometimes washed from trees and other surfaces by rainstorms. When that happens, the runoff water adds those acids to the acid rain, making the combination more acidic than the falling rain alone. The combination of acid rain plus dry deposited acid is called acid deposition. Prevailing winds transport the compounds, sometimes hundreds of miles, across states. Acid rain causes acidification of lakes and streams and contributes to damage of trees at high elevations.

In addition, acid rain accelerates the decay of building materials and paints, including irreplaceable buildings, statues, and sculptures that are part of "a nation's" cultural heritage. Prior to falling to the earth, SO_2 and NO_x gases and their particulate matter derivatives, sulfates, and nitrates contribute to visibility degradation and impact public health. While calculating the acidification indicator, several indicators exist for acidification, the most common reference substances being hydrogen ions and sulfur dioxide. Either can be expressed in terms of the other. Here we use SO_2 as the reference chemical. The method for calculating the acidification index is similar in approach to other impact indicators: the LCI substances that are present in Table 3.7 below are multiplied by the equivalency factor for the acidification potential (AP) to arrive at SO_2 equivalent quantities. The SO_2 equivalents for each life cycle stage are summed to calculate the acidification index. The following equation outlines the calculation: Acidification Index = Σi wi x APi, where wi = weight of inventory flow i per functional unit of product. APi = Acidification Potential Equivalency Factor = weight of SO_2 with the same potential acidifying effect as a unit weight of inventory flow.

Life Cycle Assessment 37

3.16 RESOURCE DEPLETION

Resource depletion is related to the inputs of materials into the industrial system under study. Although resource depletion is identified as a single environmental issue for the purposes of environmentally preferable purchasing, in fact, resource depletion is an umbrella term for several sub-issues, which collectively can be considered of equal importance as all the remaining environmental issues related to emissions. Resource depletion directly measures the sustainability of industrial systems. If resources are being used at or below their replacement rate, then their use does not affect the ability of future generations to maintain their quality of life. An example of a material used which has sustainable resource is preferred for its consumption. It was discussed in the earlier chapters. Resource depletion impact values can be presented as a single value or as sub-values that represent each of the major types of resources being consumed. Limestone is the single major resource for the cement sector; hence it was the only substance considered.

3.17 LAND USE

Land transformation is the process of changing aspects of biodiversity and life support functions (e.g., flora and fauna) from initial state to altered state. The altered state, which may represent higher or lower quality, is a temporary one. After the termination of human activity, the flora and fauna may undergo a certain degree of recovery. The difference between the initial and final steady state is the transformation impact. The transformation impact is measured in units of area (m^2). Land occupation refers to the time during which the land is unavailable for other uses (i.e., the duration of change of quality and how long the altered state is maintained). It includes both duration of human land use and time taken for a new steady state to be reached (i.e., recovery time).

The occupational impact represents the temporary changes in quality of an area of land. Units are given in terms of m^2 yr. Resource depletion/mineral depletion refers to material consumption through the product manufacturing. The Guinee and Huijengs method is used to characterize this impact. Elemental analysis is done for each of the materials accounted for, followed by multiplication with corresponding characterization factor. The final amount of material used is expressed in the kg antimony equivalents. This characterization method is chosen as it considers the ultimate reserves and rates of extraction only.

3.18 NORMALIZATION

Normalization is defined as the calculation of the magnitude of indicator results relative to a reference situation. The reference situation may relate to a given community, person, or other system, over a given period time. Other reference

38   Life Cycle Assessment

situations may be adopted; future target situations may also be adopted. The main aim of normalizing the indicator results is to better understand the relative importance and magnitude of these results for each product system. Normalization can also be used for checking inconsistencies, to provide and communicate information on the relative significance of the category results, and to prepare for additional procedures such as weighting or interpretation. Commonly, normalization is adopted at a single-scale level (i.e., the reference values taken correspond to the world).

3.19   UNCERTAINTY ANALYSIS

In this analysis, empirical data on uncertain ranges of specific data are used to calculate the total error range of the results. To assess the robustness of the results, information is required on both validity and reliability. This analysis is performed to account for whether appropriate (correct representativeness in space, time, technology, etc.), process data (sources), and models have been used. In the interpretation, the analyst looks for significant environmental aspects (e.g., energy use, greenhouse gases, and dust level), significant contributions to indicators or scores, and significant unit processes in the system. For example, if the results of an impact assessment indicate a particularly high value for the GWP indicator, the analyst could refer to the inventory to determine which outputs are contributing to the high value, and which unit processes those outputs are coming from. This is also used as a form of quality control. It helps provide more certain conclusions and recommendations. The procedure typically involves examination of the sensitivity of results, performance of a scenario analysis, a review data quality, and a comparison of the results to the original goals of the study.

Decision-making for industrial activities, both in terms of government policy and the decisions of companies, faces an increasingly challenging task in recent decades. Production systems become more complex and automated in response to rapid globalization and advancing process and management technologies. Societies face complex choices in the pursuit of sustainable industrial development. The global production system of goods and services becomes more extensive under the influence of globalization and technological change. Sustainable development sets forth an agenda including economic, environmental, and social objectives, which are often difficult to satisfy simultaneously. Considering these points, analysis of and information systems for industrial activities must evolve to constructively inform decision-making.

3.20   INTERPRETATION

Interpretation is the final phase of an LCA. In the interpretation, the analyst looks for significant environmental aspects (e.g., energy use, greenhouse gases), significant

Life Cycle Assessment

contributions to indicators or scores, and significant unit processes in the system. For example, if the results of an impact assessment had indicated a particularly high value for the GWP indicator, the analyst could refer to the inventory to determine which outputs are contributing to the high value, and from which unit processes those outputs are coming. This is also used as a form of quality control. It helps provide more certain conclusions and recommendations. The procedure typically involves examination of the sensitivity of results, performance of a scenario analysis, a review data quality, and a comparison of the results to the original goals of the study.

When studying a single product or when improvements relate only to the production process or phase, when comparing products with the same function, a definition of this function is necessary. Subsequently, you need to identify the consequences of such a definition for the product or process description. In practice it has been observed that initially one should spend relatively more time formulating the scope upon starting a new LCA. The goal definition is meant to give an overview of the premises of the study. When there is no overview at the first stage, try to formulate the ideas briefly and roughly and then later adjust them, if necessary. When the goal definition has been completed, continue the study by making the inventory analysis. This means that one needs to proceed stage by stage by drawing up a process flowchart, collecting data, defining the system boundaries, and processing the data, which should be executed iteratively. Keeping in view the various impact categories, Figure 3.4 shows a model of acidification impact using a category indicator (proton release H^+ aq.) and its impact on the endpoint.

3.21 CLASSIFICATION

In the first step of classification, impact categories of interest are identified in the scoping phase of the LCA. Broadly, there are four major heads: the categories are natural resource impacts, abiotic ecosystem impacts, potential human health, and ecotoxicity impacts. LCA is a holistic yardstick of environmental performance. The method is a science-based assessment of the environmental impacts of products and services. LCA captures relevant environmental impacts from cradle to grave, thereby providing comprehensive information on such issues as ecological, climate change, land use, and resource depletion. LCA is a flexible tool that provides vital support in environmental decision-making. Several documents developed under the auspices of the ISO (ISO 14040 series) describe the general LCA approach and the issues that are involved in conducting LCA. These standards have established a worldwide recognition of LCA as an important and viable environmental management tool. LCA provides the basis of an informed approach to environmental decision-making. Thus, those working with life cycle issues, even in different sectors, can learn much from each other about ways of organizing and benefiting from LCA work. The construction industry shows that

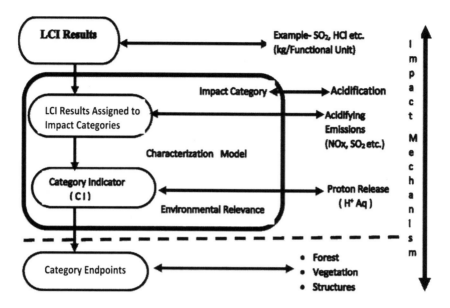

FIGURE 3.4 Life cycle impact categories.

TABLE 3.7
Impact Assessment of Different Building Materials

Impact Assessment	Clay Bricks (thousands)	Aggregates (1 tonne)	Cement (1 tonne)	Ready Mix Concrete (1 m³)	Steel (1 tonne)	Aluminum (1 tonne)
GWP kg/tonne (CO_2-Eq.)	400	2.0	1200	0.25	3000	5699
AP (SO_2-Eq.)	0.23	0.011	1.65	0.56	6.63	7.4

LCA results can help in making decisions, whereas on the other hand, the environmentally best solution may retard developmental activities. To get best possible alternative path efforts, one needs to have all possible inputs and outputs to inform the impact assessment. LCA is simply a way to stop the never-ending journey to reducing emissions. In construction, the use of materials plays a pivotal role in various environmental impacts. Table 3.7 shows the two environmental impacts of different building materials, a comparison that can help to select the best materials to use.

It is interesting to observe that in one of the LCA studies, four commercial buildings in India in different climate zones were selected for the study. Table 3.8

TABLE 3.8
Details of Four Commercial Buildings

NO s.	Commercial Building	Type/ Usage	Land Area (m²)	Constructed Area (m²)	Open Area (m²)	Pavement Area (m²)	Area for Parking (m²)	Gardening Area (m²)	No. of Floors	No. of Units
1	Gurgaon	Official	4382	15885	1970	1922	6652	37	3B+G+8 (Tower& 3B+G+3 (Non-Tower)	2
2	Chennai	IT Park	161850	797893	107107	80625	222638	26482	2B+G+11/ 3B+G+9	9
3	Kolkata	IT Park	104812	258012	70889	26212	18464	26212	B+G+11	7
4	Hyderabad	IT Park	106128	374642	63660	26540	149058	6540	2B+G+15	4

42   Life Cycle Assessment

TABLE 3.9
Impact Assessment of Typical Commercial Building

Impact Category	Unit	Total	Construction Phase	Building Operation	Building Maintenance	Demolition Phase
Global warming (GWP 100)	kg CO$_2$ eq	7760.92	487.10	7167.93	54.94	50.95
Ozone layer depletion (ODP)	kg CFC -11 eq	1.64E-05	1.85E-06	4.58E-06	1.81E-06	8.19E-06
Photochemical oxidation	kg C$_2$H$_4$	3.42	0.22	3.12	0.03	0.05
Acidification	kg SO$_2$ eq	101.56	2.29	98.70	0.23	0.34
Eutrophication	kg PO$_4$ eq	8.13	0.23	7.82	0.02	0.07
Nonrenewable, fossil	MJ eq	14,349.00	986.55	11,912.98	178.61	1270.85

TABLE 3.10
Comparison of Cement Having Different Percentages of Fly Ash

Impact category	Unit	OPC	PPC_25% FA	PPC_30% FA	PPC_35% FA	OPC_ 40% FA	OPC_50% FA
GWP	kg CO$_2$ eq	1033.71	795.26	747.57	700.06	651.11	556.99
POCP	kg C$_2$H$_4$	0.12	0.10	0.10	0.09	0.09	0.08
AP	kg SO$_2$ eq	4.33	3.49	3.32	3.16	2.99	2.65
EP	kg PO$_4$-- eq	0.48	0.38	0.36	0.34	0.32	0.28
Nonrenewable	MJ eq	702.61	703.89	704.14	707.06	706.55	707.82

depicts details of commercial buildings of four different cities, three of them are IT parks and one of them is an office building. A detailed LCA study was carried out. Table 3.9 gives six impact categories of different phases during construction of a commercial building, including the construction phase, building operation, building maintenance, and building demolition. It is remarkable that the operation phase has maximum impact out of various environmental parameters. Table 3.10 shows clearly that if cement (OPC) is replaced by fly ash in different percentages for PPC cement, it can have a lot of advantages in reducing environmental impacts. In the comparison of different types of cement without compromising with quality on long run, there is much advantage in reducing major environmental impacts.

4 Life Cycle Tools

4.1 LIFE CYCLE ASSESSMENT: ENVIRONMENT

Life Cycle Assessment (LCA) provides a systematic scientific approach to quantifying resource consumption and environmental releases to air, water, and soil associated with products, processes, and services. It takes into consideration all product life cycle stages from extracting and processing raw materials, manufacturing, transportation and distribution, use/reuse, and recycling and waste management to access the environmental and economic impacts. LCA is a decision-making tool for governments and businesses. It is used to measure and compare the environmental impacts of products and services, frequently using computer-modeling software. Most LCA measurements will be made by summing the units of energy consumed in the extraction of raw materials, transport, manufacture, distribution, and final disposal of a product or service.

The application of LCA in different organizations can be useful for various purposes. It can support decision-making in product and process development and be used for monitoring the environmental performance of products. It can help with strategic planning for continual environmental improvement. It also has a marketing purpose, namely, ecolabeling. It can also help in the selection of subcontractors in supply chain. Using LCA for the growth of an enterprise, one application that can trigger another that is inside gain from an LCA into product and environmental performance can lead to decision about selection of suppliers. It is also seen that LCA has traditionally been developed as a tool to be used as a product leveling. There is an increasing interest in using LCA at the corporate level to reflect the performance of various individual plants in a life cycle perspective, which is particularly relevant for large enterprises and for application related to monitoring of environmental performance and strategic planning for image building.

The use of LCA to document and monitor environmental performance at a corporate level is today often limited to few selected impact categories, including, typically GHG, acidification potential, human toxicity, and footprint indicators like carbon and water. At the product level, LCA is often used during product development and for identifying environmental hot spots of a product or process either within the organization or in its supply chain. For instance, until 1990, LCA was used internally to identify hot spots in products and systems and for process optimization. Other enterprises used LCA during the 1990s to set up new priorities for changes in products and processes, such as saving or substituting materials. In parallel to its application in product and process development, LCA is often used for marketing purposes at various levels. Currently, LCA addresses economic and social issues in the struggle to achieve sustainability goals.

As public concerns about the state of the environment have become increasingly pronounced and consumers are more demanding and environmentally conscious,

DOI: 10.1201/9781003206750-4

44   Life Cycle Assessment

enterprises have also placed a larger focus on quantifying their environmental performance, using LCA and communicating results to publicly brand their enterprise as "green." "Green" and "climate change" are two buzzwords for all activities of society. Most of the company's expectation for the use of LCA is not to get a competitive advantage but to increase the company's image or reputation in contributing for environmental excellence. It helps in mitigating climate change for sustainability. Ecolabels or environmental product declarations can establish good environmental performance and be used to make a given product more appealing for environmentally conscious consumers.

In the future, together with the development of guidelines of the organization's environmental footprint, the corporate-level industry will also use LCA for setting strategic objectives; some of the companies may also carry out studies to better understand their environmental performance to implement environmental management system. LCA is a tool to implement a structured program of a continual improvement in environmental performance and to manage communication and an enterprise's environmental performance internally and externally. There is thus often a relationship between the implementation of EMS and the implementation of LCA within a company.

4.2 LIFE CYCLE COSTING

Life cycle assessment deals with environmental aspects, whereas life cycle costing (LCC) accounts for economic aspects, but both share common features and objectives. It is to assess the impact over the whole life cycle of a process of all product and present information in a manner that supports the decision-making process. But the purpose of an LCC exercise is usually to integrate the total capital and operating cost and its components over extended periods and then to present the figures as a relative value that can easily be compared and assessed against alternative tools. LCC does not explicitly deal with environmental impact, although it can frequently be used to support environmentally sensitive impacts and their resolution, specially where the operating and maintenance costs are significant. It has many similarities with LCA, and there is potential use in combining LCA with LCC. The key similarities are that both LCC and LCA use data on qualities of materials used, service life of the materials used for maintenance, and operational impacts of using the product. But in the end-of-life proportion to recycling and disposal, such a combination has been realized to integrate LCC with LCA. It is particularly important to show the relation between design choices and resulting costs of energy and maintenance and operating costs including cleaning of buildings. Cleaning costs are often higher than the energy costs. Still few inventories on cleaning products are available. While in many cases, they must be using cleaning products much higher than their actual requirement without adopting appropriate methodology.

Discounting distinguishes LCC from LCA in which an environmental impact occurring in the future can have the same significance as that occurring in the present. Discount rates are considered acceptable in the LCC. To perform this

Life Cycle Tools 45

assessment, it is necessary to produce an inventory of the yearly total cost. It includes the capital maintenance operational cost in considering energy saving measures adopted. It is one of the simple ways of considering the cost of additional capital investment reduction in the payback period. It entails defining the amount of time it will take to recover the initial investment in energy saving and dividing the initial installation cost by the annual energy cost saving. While simple payback is easy to compute, its weakness is that it fails to factor in the time value of the money, inflation, and the project's lifetime operational and maintenance costs.

Although these techniques are widely appreciated, the application of these techniques to real construction project chief gives little attention. Data for capital costs of components and service are widely available but obtaining data for operating costs can be a challenging task. Obtaining real data for, say, building operations and maintenance costs is a problem because they are widely considered commercially confidential. Components and systems that reduce building environmental impacts are frequently associated with reducing life cycle resources and hence usually with reducing running costs. The essential element of an LCC exercise is to consider the energy cost of all options, particularly where the proposed solution improves the energy efficiency of the building because energy prices can be expected to be significant during the life cycle of the building. It is important that costs are assessed on the basis of rational forecast statistics as well as current prices using a number of energy price scenarios will assert in-house team of the building management system; to ascertain the future price rises an understanding of the sensitivity of the building to future price increase potential more important than trying through activate an accurate forecast of energy, such a combination has been realized. It is particularly important to show the relation between the design choices, and resulting utility costs for energy reduction, maintenance, operating, and cleaning costs are often higher than the energy cost. But there are few inventories which are maintained.

4.3   SOCIAL LIFE CYCLE ASSESSMENT

The goal of sustainable development is human well-being, contributing to the needs of current and future generations. Most of the leading organizations through, inter alia, a policy instrument are having global strategy supported by methodology and techniques and tools which can contribute to sustainability objective. In the field of product and process assessment, some methods have been developed recently, in which it includes policies and strategies for the social economic aspects in the environmental dimension of sustainable development. But in recent years several efforts have been pursued to cover in a more coherent and integrated way all pillars of sustainable development. It is within this context that these aspects have been perceived, such as when consumers ask themselves about the social and economic circumstances under which a product is made. Enterprises do not want to be linked to, for example, child labor or corruption either within the organization or in the supply chain. Trade unions want to show solidarity with their fellow workers.

Public authorities need to apply integrated product policy that is in place, for example, in public procurement. Governments should ensure that all stakeholders know that goods and services are produced in a sustainable way. When considering products and services in terms of sustainable development, a life cycle perspective brings powerful insights. It aims to provide increased knowledge of the three-pillars approach of sustainable development that considers people, the planet, and profit, taking into account prosperity along the whole supply chain from extraction of raw materials to the end of a product's life. This all meant to inform more comprehensive decision-making. There are two tools that have been developed to assess part of this framework, the most famous being the environmental life cycle assessment (ELCA). ELCA assesses the impact of economic activity on the natural environment, and to a lesser extent on human health and natural resources. Life cycle costing, discussed earlier, is a tool that primarily focuses on the direct cost and benefit from the economic activity for people, the planet, and profit. Until now no commonly accepted methodology was available for internally and externally assessing the production of goods and services. It is precisely what this tool presents is to deliver a way to assess the product based on social and social economic indicators using the most current available state-of-the-art methods. Integrating the ELCA and the LCC, it is complementing in contributing full assessment of goods and service within the context of sustainable development. In the guidelines of life cycle assessment in reference to 1993, a code of practice was established by SETAC/UNEP. At the beginning of 2010, some research groups presented their methodologies for cradle-to-grave assessment of goods and service with social criteria. Some of these methodologies were branded as SLCA studies. In some of the methodologies, social issues were referred, while others have gone one step further. By presenting such social LCA at the same time, similar exercises were also undertaken in parallel by different research groups of the worlds; as a result, several social assessment tools were surfaced. It was motivated to include the use of LCA in developing countries, but due to lack of expertise and data availability, social aspects were not be able to include. In LCA studies in developing countries, some key social issues generated negative perception. It can be anti-development-oriented, because it provides only a picture of negative and more cognitive consequences but does not reflect any of the positive aspects of the development, namely, social and economic benefits. Even if the value of LCA is appreciated, a justification for excessive cost is lacking since it does not address the developing countries. But of late it is now picking up extremely fast in developing countries.

Most significant concerns, that is, poverty eradication together with the social aspects such as employment rates, wages, accidents, and working conditions, and human rights were expressed. UNEP through one of its task force the aim were expressed follows to convert the current environmental tool LCA into triple bottom line sustainable development tool to establish a framework for all the country inclusion of socio economic benefit into LCA to determine the implication of LCIA to provide an international forum for the setting of experience with integration of social aspect into LCA. It is not a new absorption that nearly every society is

Life Cycle Tools

supported by an environmental, a social and economic pillar. The interconnection among the three pillars has been emphasized over the last few decades. Several analyses also refer to art and cultural damage to societies. Within the context of these guidelines, it is not possible to perform an in-depth review, so a society is developing socially and economically within an environmentally conditioned context. All underlined aspects are at least of some importance for the functioning of the society. Today, the current level of awareness of the interconnection among these several aspects is not adequate for optimal decision-making. Much too often decisions are made based only on political and economic factors without considering the environmental or social criteria and cultural differences. And yet for some time, now methodological frameworks have been developed by scientists to measure changes or transformation in parts of society in a holistic and integrated way. During the last two decades those frameworks have been placed within the context of sustainable development. The concept, within which SLCA was developed and applied, includes the following concept of sustainable development, human well-being, and sustainable consumption and production, along with the life cycle thinking-related techniques for product and process assessment.

Environmental life cycle assessment normally referred to as life cycle assessment is a technique that aims at addressing the environmental aspect of a product and their potential and mental impacts throughout the product's life cycle. The term *product* refers to both goods and services. A product cycle includes all stages of a product system from raw material acquisition or natural resource production to the disposal of the product at the end of its life, including extracting and processing of raw material manufacturing distribution use, reuse maintenance, recycling, and final disposal. The four major phases of ELCA consist, as in LCA and SLCA of goal and scope setting, inventory analysis, impact assessment, and interpretation.

There are two types of consideration when orientation is suggested to earthy assessment of social and, to some extent, economic aspects and technical consideration. The orientation has engulfed and discussed through three topics: one is the definition of social impacts, second one is the classification of social and social economic indicators, and third one is the development of subcategory of social and socioeconomic impact assessment of products. Social impacts are consequences of positive or negative pressures on social endpoints, that is, the well-being of stakeholders.

Because of this complexity and this subjectivity, it is not recommended to define attributes of relationships unilaterally and from there define sets of related indicators isolated from stakeholder contexts. As for the environmental impact, the doubt expressed by climate change deniers, defining social impact categories needs to go through a subjective and intersubjective process is, preferred. It can also ensure the comprehensiveness of the framework. The purpose of classification into impact categories is to support the identification of stakeholders to classify subcategory indicators within groups that have same impact and to support further impact assessment and interpretation. The impact category should preferably reflect internationally recognized categorization standards.

48 Life Cycle Assessment

However, efforts will have to be made while conducting SLCA to find and redefine the appropriate indicators to assist the subcategories adapted to the context and understanding. The first thing needed when initiating a SLCA is a clear statement of the purpose and goal. This statement describes the intended use and pursuit. The study will then be defined to meet that purpose, within any constraints. Depending on the goal, a critical review may be planned. The second step is to define the scope. Defining the scope, the function and the functional unit of the product are crucial. Based on that information the product system will later be modeled using process input–output data.

The scope is also defined in the first phase of the study; it encompasses issues of depth and breadth of the study. It defines the limits placed on the product life cycle, which ideally exist on the border between the economy and nature. The detailed information is to be collected and analyzed. It must be ensured that from where the data will be coming from, how up to date this study will be, how information will be handled, and where results will be applicable. ISO 14040-2006 states that the scope should be sufficiently well defined to ensure that the breadth and depth and detail of the study are compatible and sufficient to address the stated goal. The process chains in LCA model provide a valuable starting point to this system scope of SLCA. The process chain provides the details of the series of operation performed in the making, treatment use, and disposal of a product. Process chain is built with base and economic input and output supplemented with the amount of data available. The economic input and output method considers an entire economy, including all activities of all industry sectors, but the processes are exaggerated. On the other hand, the process methodology covers detailed information on specific processes, but important parts of the product system may be left out because of the difficulty of following the entire supply chain in detail. It is necessary to specify the function and functional unit in SLCA. As stated in ISO 14044-2006, the scope clearly specifies the functional performance characteristics of the system being studied for its utility. The outcome of the study of the product helps to inform consumers. Modeling the product system is essential to identifying locations and specific stakeholders involved. It is also important in estimating the needs and targets for site-specific data collection. When using qualitative indicators and data in SLCA it may be difficult to link the results specifically to the functional unit it is still necessary though we define the function unit product utility in the goal and scope of the case of the study as this provides the necessary basis for the product system modeling. To help define a valuable functional unit five steps are essential: (1) describe the product and its properties, (2) determine the product's social utility, (3) determine the relevant market segment, (4) determine the relevant product alternates, and (5) determine the reference flow for each of the product systems.

In SLCA, the definition of the function needs to consider both technical and social acceptability of the product, such as functionality (referring to the main function), technical quality (such as stability and durability), ease of maintenance, services rendered during use and disposal, aesthetics (such as appearance and design), and images of the product; the total costs are related to purchase,

Life Cycle Tools 49

use, and disposal. The criteria to determine a product property is to be included in the functional unit. The function one needs must be the function that two products to be compared may differ, but the functional unit must be the same. Of course, the difference function makes assessment weaker, but the functional unit must be the same. The function you need must be based on outcome and not on the item especially when the goal is to be compared between two products. One of the primary purposes of the functional unit is to provide a reference to which the input and output data can be normalized in a mathematical sense. Therefore, the functional unit should be clearly defined and measurable, and the functional limit should also be consistent with the goal and scope of the study. ISO 14044-2006 defines the reference flow as a measure of the output from the processes in each product system required to fulfill the functional expression by the functional unit.

4.4 LIFE CYCLE SUSTAINABILITY ASSESSMENT

The world has undergone a paradigm shift from environmental protection towards sustainability. Sustainability does not only focus on environmental impacts, but consists of the three dimensions, including the environment, economy, and social well-being, for which society needs to find a balance. Sustainability has become mainstream in present activities. It is accepted by all stakeholders of corporate houses, multinational companies, government, small-scale industry, and NGOs. Unfortunately, this collective understanding merely relates to a general concept rather than proactive actions by all. If we want to make sustainability happen as a concrete reality in both public policy making and corporate strategy, it needs strong commitment. To make it happen, we must be positive and strong will to do. Now most of corporations and major industries and organizations are taking positive steps for sustainability. The life cycle perspective considers for products all life cycle stages and for organizations the complete supply or value chains, from raw material extraction and acquisition, through energy and material production and manufacturing, to use and end-of-life treatment and final disposal. Another important principle is comprehensiveness because it considers that all attributes are aspects of environmental, economic, and social issues. By considering all attributes and aspects within one assessment in a cross-media and multidimensional perspective, potential tradeoffs can be identified and assessed. LCA and life cycle management has a pivotal role to play. LCA is the internationally accepted method of measuring environmental performance. The pioneering work was done by a SETAC working group. Based on the broad acceptance of the documented work done by SETAC/UNEP (United Nations Environmental Programme) on the life cycle initiative, the following scheme for life cycle sustainability assessment represents as LCSA = LCA + LCC + SLCA. The UNEP and SETAC launched the life cycle initiative to enable users around the world to put LCT into practice and introduce life cycle management as one of their areas of work, in which measurement of the environmental parameters of sustainability with LCA is well-established tool; a similar approach was developed more recently for the economy: LCC.

This development is crucial because it fosters the opportunity of life cycle-based sustainability assessments.

Based on the definition for life cycle management and sustainability development, it is suggested that accordingly life cycle sustainability management can be defined as a strategic management system that aims at minimizing an organization's negative impact on the natural and social environment by its product or services. The entire product/service life cycle and value chain assure that natural social and economic resources are sustained for future generation. This definition calls for close collaboration between stakeholders along the value chain and also interaction with stakeholders who represent the natural and social environment. Figure 4.1 explains LCSA using a triangle indicating the relationship with the environment based on life cycle assessment (LCA), prosperity estimated through life cycle costing (LCC), and finally social life cycle assessment (SLCA), covering people's benefits. In the center of the triangle LCSA covers the three aspects of environment, society, and economy.

The idea of LCSA builds on the so-called three pillars composed of environmental, social, and economic pillars; the interpretation gained momentum in the concept of triple bottom line. It is proposed that business should manage environmental, social, and economic aspects of sustainability in the same feature in two ways, that is, financial aspects are typically managed in accounting. LCC is an abbreviation for life cycle costing which aimed to quantify all costs associated with life cycle of a product that is directly covered by one or more of the actors in the life cycle. LCC and SLCA are especially important to integrate with LCA. An important requirement of LCSA is that the three pillars

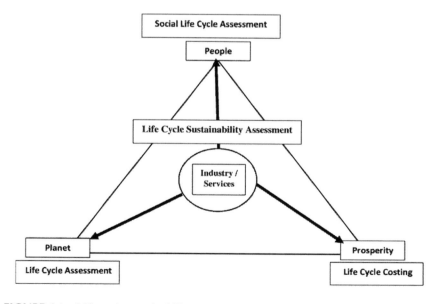

FIGURE 4.1 Life cycle sustainability assessment.

of sustainability must be assessed using same system boundary and the same element of product life cycle in all three assessments. While LCSA is much less mature than LCA and there is little agreement how to perform it, LCSA seems to assume that sustainability is something that can be balanced between the environmental, social, and economic dimensions. Sustainability has become the most common approach to development in the last three decades, entering the discourse in numerous disciplines at all levels. Researchers, government institutions at all levels of business, and civil society organizations all have their own interpretation of the concept. Figure 4.2 illustrates the life cycle impacts and sustainability system in the form of a model. The figure explains how environmental aspects and their impacts move outward for multistakeholders and how the impact of industry is not confined to a site, but rather moves beyond the boundary from local to regional to global, which engulfs social issues, economical aspects, and environmental impacts.

4.5 ORGANIZATIONAL LIFE CYCLE ASSESSMENT

Organization Life Cycle Assessment (OLCA) has been promoted as a robust quantitative tool like LCA in normal decision-making. While LCA was originally developed of for products, the benefits of the life cycle approach may be extended to the more complex prospect of organizational assessment. Within this context, the unit life cycle initiative launched the flexible tool life cycle assessment of an organization to further explore the capability and applicability. OLCA uses a life cycle perspective to satisfy and evaluate the input, output, and potential environmental impacts of activity associated with an organization. This methodology can serve multiple goals at the same time, identifying environmental hot spots throughout the value chain, tracking the environmental performance, supporting strategic decisions, and informing corporate sustainability reporting. One goal that OLCA cannot currently fulfill is externally communicating comparisons between different organizations. Comparative assertion is neither robust nor meaningful due to lack of consistent basis for comparison. But it is envisioned for organizations of all sizes, both public and private, in all sectors, and all over

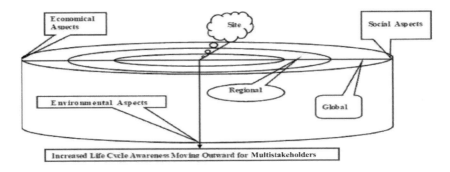

FIGURE 4.2 Life cycle and sustainability system.

the world. The first tentative steps towards full OLCA application are currently taking place and the outcome of these are already being used to improve organizations' environmental performance. Broadening the base of implementation, the logical next step is requiring accessible, practical guidelines and guidance. Three different pathways describe how organizations with previous experience with environmental tools can use this as a basis to think bigger and take an integrated and holistic approach. Additionally specific recommendation for small, medium, and large is to provide practical way forward. The direction is given for several situations that there is no one-size-fits-all application of OLCA. The experience of few first mover illustrates that the process and benefit of applying environmental multi-impact assessment of organization are increasingly recognizing that they need to understand their environmental impacts at all levels including those throughout their value chain. Companies are engaging with partners along the entire value chain to assist the opportunity for efficiency, increase competitiveness, and assess new markets as well as strengthen their capacity to respond to risks such as those emerging from taking positive steps for reduction of resources and climate change. Governments too are feeling a growing pressure to become more sustainable through sustainable purchasing decisions in their public procurement and more broadly throughout their activity.

All organizations have a vital role to play in efforts to reduce environmental impacts: large corporations due to their relative share of resource depletion and polluting and toxic emissions, and small and medium-sized enterprises (SMEs) due to their collective impact. Therefore, static decisions with long-term implications should no longer be based merely on technical and economic considerations. For organizations to take credible steps towards protection of the environment, industry needs stable schemes to frame its approaches. In view of this, at the 2002 World Summit for Sustainable Development in Johannesburg, there was a call for a comprehensive set of programs focusing on sustainable conjunction and production. Several methodologies, tools, and techniques are available for organizations to assess, compare, and show the environmental performance of their products, including goods and services.

At the organizational level, all approach for many organizations in the EMS could be satisfied by ISO 14001's equal management and audit schemes. They are procedural tools, and when including an organizing eco balance, they commonly analyze only get-to-get process more over the past organizational environmental analysis approach. For example, carbon footprinting of corporations was proposed with the greenhouse gas protocol initiatives WRI and WBCSD 2004, 2011, and ISO 14069. Another example of carbon disclosure projects is CDP 2014. In addition, they mostly concentrate on single environmental aspects and indicators and hence have not followed an environmental multi-impact approach. It should be acknowledged though that these methodologies have been promoted and assessed to a certain extent, but it needs the application in an organizational context.

LCA is a scientific methodology to support sustainable production and consumption patterns. LCA considers a comprehensive setup and environmental

Life Cycle Tools

aspects and potential impacts of a product over its entire life cycle from raw material extraction through material processing, manufacture, distribution, use, repair, maintenance, disposal, and recycling. It has been supported and promoted by the UNEP/SETAC Life Cycle Initiative among others for developing countries as a robust quantity to tool for decision-making by producers and other stakeholders. Many private and public sector organizations, multinational companies, and various state and central governments have already committed to improve the social environmental performance by adapting life cycle approaches. Many consumers are already using life cycle information to make purchase decisions. The benefits and potential lessons from the life cycle perspective are not limited to products. Nevertheless, the assessment of an organization is often more complex than that of products. There is more than one product life cycle performer since most organizations are engaged in many products' life cycles to different degrees, having many departments and business divisions. Additionally, a large part of the environmental impact may effect outside the organization. Because many assorted products and sectors converge into one organization, the range of waste and by-products can be huge. Environmental performance of organizations including activity up and down the value chain, mostly focusing on GHG emissions, reveal that life cycle resource use and emissions could significantly contribute to the environmental performance of organizations.

5 Guidance for Life Cycle Inventory

5.1 LIFE CYCLE INVENTORIES

Today, technologies and processes are advancing at breakneck speeds for various products and services that have become increasingly diverse in their sources of materials, manufacturing, assembly locations, areas of use, and points of final disposition. To accurately reflect this diversity, data must be available for areas where the activity embodied in a life cycle assessment takes place. When one talks about LCA data, the focus is on Life Cycle Inventory (LCI) data, although characterizing factors associated with the LCIA method are often included in LCA databases. The technical basis from the practice of LCA has become more standardized and as more decisions are supported with the methodology demand for high quality documented transparent independently reviewed, data increases tremendously in different countries. Applications of carbon and water footprinting also can be supported by these LCA data because LCA data include all environmental emissions and conjunctions. Coordinated global efforts to define and produce high-quality LCA data are required if LCA practice is to advance in the most scientific manner. Furthermore, a similar effort on data interchange is required to allow for a maximum exchange of information among LCA practitioners of different countries. In a global economy, how well product and services are sourced from many countries? Databases as a repository of this information are being established at a rapid pace. Data sets contained within the system must meet increasingly rigorous criteria if they are to be consistent and exchangeable among users worldwide.

Only with the widespread availability of healthy information will society be able to make efficient and effective decisions on policies and design options that will allow future generations to meet their own needs and aspirations. A life cycle management framework for the environmental sustainability of products describes the strategy to achieve this sustainability from the basis of an overall vision that is supported by life cycle management systems and policies. These strategies are achieved through implementation and execution of the program and activities like design of the environment, green procurement, and recycling. This is achieved when the vision of green economy results in the reality of sustainable consumption and production patterns through resource efficiency. All these system program activities are made operational by tools such as LCA and other life cycle approaches, which need appropriate data most easily provided by reliable databases. Access is to credible information on the potential life cycle environmental impacts of a product is especially crucial when we attempt to

DOI: 10.1201/9781003206750-5

56 Life Cycle Assessment

communicate the preferable environmental characteristics of a product and hence make a green claim to influence institutional and individual consumers to purchase products while considering their environmental footprints.

While this guidance provides a range of specific benefits to other actors, one of the major benefits is the understanding of their roles in the data chain and what expectations they should have from the database manager regarding data development, review, and use. It is expected that those actors in data supply roles will especially appreciate the clarity this guidance brings to the requirement and expectation of the data submitted for the assembly of data sets, particularly on the recommended associated documentation. Using the general data collection method in ISO 14040 and ISO 14044 is the starting point. This section proposes the following steps: (1) prepare an inventory list of inputs and outputs, (2) define the mathematical relationships, (3) collect the raw data, (4) perform the calculations, (5) provide other supporting information. The developer also should document relevant data and information for validation, review, and update purposes. Data set end users, like practitioner, create LCA, a model with the respective data sets into mathematical relationship. One has to process raw data and supportive information. In order to have completeness, a list of inputs and outputs of the unit process is needed before data are collected. This list needs to be in accordance with the goal and scope and can be prepared using various steps for product, and all imports such as material energy service input should always be included in inventory list.

5.2 DATA COLLECTION

Guidance to the user on the process is of data collection, including not only method of data collection but also suggestions on which data collection method to apply in which situation and how to deal with the missing data and insight into the documentation that is required. Data collection is the process of gathering data for specific purpose. Data collection provides the data needed to complete a unit process data set, but it also covers what is needed for quality assurance benchmark comparisons and other similar data. It is linked to the process modeling the application of the mathematical relationship where process modeling tells that data are needed, and data collection is the process of locating the needed data. This activity may overlap especially when data collection involves the calculation of missing data. Data collection has also supported validation by collecting and comparing raw data and inventory data. There are several ways to obtain useful data. Interviews compile a complete list of flow diagrams of detail processing that must be considered and addressed by process head of the plant. Develop a simple questionnaire as clear and as short as possible for collection of data. Perform statistical analysis for quality checks. Make sure that the result is representative of the definition and size of the sample. Data collectors should be aware of the impact of the utility of the collected information. It is good practice to use a group approach to organize the work in data collection where data owners and data collectors collaborate. As an example, trade association often is good group to task

Guidance for Life Cycle Inventory

with the data collection because they will have expertise in the process and the environmental regulatory requirements.

5.3 DOCUMENTATION AND REVIEW

Databases are intended to organize, store, and retrieve large amounts of digital LCI data sets easily. They consist of an organized collection of LCI data sets. The database will allow for interconnection if confirmed to a common set of criteria including methodology. The computer result can be used with identified LCIA methods for life cycle assessment. Databases are managed using database management system that store database content, allowing data creation and maintenance. In contrast, a data set's very life is a collection of data sets that may not conform to common criteria and does not allow for interconnection and common application of LCA or LCIA purposes. An example of a data set library is the UNEP/SETAC database registry. It is a specific LCA database that would cover situations where the data sets are looking at only limited interventions such as carbon. These data bases follow the same criteria for general purpose LCI databases but with a narrower scope. Each data set must have one of the following-functional unit in case of a partial product system with defined use which need not be quantified as a flow but can be any quantified use that is meter square-references flow indicators of a single output are allocated processes.

Finally, to facilitate review a sensitivity analysis is recommended. Life cycle assessment should use the most appropriate data set and modeling approaches to meet the specific goal and scope required to satisfactorily answer the questions raised. Current LCI databases are often sufficient to provide the required information to meet many consumers, industry, and government objectives. However, additional details on the current data as well as supplemental data sources will be needed to provide satisfactory answers to the emerging questions in the fields of LCA and sustainability. The continuing evolution in consumer preferences, green growth imperatives of an industry, and public policy forces continuous development and improvement of data sets and methodologies for LCA to meet these needs. The continuous development is extending data collection and modeling methods. The purpose of this is to identify the additional requirement of LCA data sets and databases to meet the evolving stakeholder needs and to fulfill the specific goal and scope of an assessment. The overall guiding principle is extended adaptive approaches. Aims to describe how environmentally relevant flow for a product system will change in response to decision on products and volume are alternate technologies in response to it changing the demand.

5.4 INPUT AND OUTPUT DATA

The compilation of input and output data as a part of national accounts by national agencies is now routine practice in different countries governed by UN standards. In the nations' average monetary terms and in each economic sector, how much one sector buys from each of the other sectors for unit produced is compiled. It

58   Life Cycle Assessment

gives an overview of the transaction; indeed, national economy and the number of sectors and the definition vary from country to country. At the national level, several countries produce input and output (IO) tables for various sectors. The United States and Japan produce IO tables with a resolution of about 500 sectors. The calculation is based on the data for industrial sectors and will thus provide results for the "average product" for the sector. The computational structure of input and output table (IOT) is functionally the same as LCA because data are used as an approximation for specific products or product group from the sector. The precision of these approximations depends on whether the study products or product group is typically of other product in this sector. The purpose of more general sustainability assessment and the environmental assessment are typically considered in LCA, but sectoral authentic environmental data are not readily available in most of the countries. In many countries the data have been collected but the environmental information system is in a fluid state.

5.5 CAPACITY BUILDING

The term *capacity building* is used with respect to a wide range of strategies and processes to create awareness of and train stakeholders to practice LCA and generate data for incentivization. When executed, these strategies end processes will contribute to a better understanding of the benefit of the quality for life cycle data, how to use these data, and how to start up, run, maintain, document, and review life cycle databases. The development of technical expertise is considered essential, especially in developing and emerging economies. Capacity building is meant to address researchers, policy makers, and industry to create a critical mass of experts in all parts of society. These increased capabilities result in a broader use of LCA and thus influence market development and the cost-benefit ratio of life cycle data management. The global life cycle assessment database guidance process, as mentioned in the introduction, is designed to provide global guidance on the establishment and maintenance of LCA databases as the basis of for future improvement in interlinking databases worldwide, facilitation of additional data generation including for certain applications such as carbon and water footprint creation, and to enhance overall data accessibility. The process also increase the credibility of existing LCA data through the provision of such guidance, especially as it relates to usability for various purposes.

In developing countries and emerging economies, because resources are lacking, international and intergovernmental organization are called upon to support the national effort hand-in-hand with essential local partners such as national life cycle networks, centers of excellence, national cleaner production centers, and industry associations. Following UN principles, sectoral and gender balance should be pursued, and they should be considered when designing the training activities. Global coordination among LCI data developers and database managers need to be identified together with capacity building and data mining as priorities in a move towards a world with interlinked databases and overall accessibility to data. There is a need for a global coordination among LCI data set developers and

Guidance for Life Cycle Inventory

database managers to ensure that these guidance principles are applied. There are vast amounts of relevant raw data and even developed LCI data sets available that are currently not easily assessable by LCA studies. LCA database managers and LCA practitioners should do data mining by working with actors who are routinely collecting data about the inputs and outputs of the unit processes and related life cycle information. Several important pathways for access to local data and national data sets should be considered.

5.6 FUTURE OUTLOOK

Future scenarios for knowledge management involve three important and independent trends that can potentially influence LCA and its handling of data and databases.

- Government, industry associations, and other database providers will take strong action to improve cooperation.
- Many new stakeholders will join the LCA community as they need more life cycle inventory data, which creates a new dynamic.
- An important revolution in the way internet communities now generate and manage data is occurring in the cloud.

Current trends in information technology will shape users' expectations regarding data, software functionality, and interoperability. These trends will also alter the scope of what can be done with LCI data in basic ways. While the LCA community should not be too distracted by these technological trends, to completely ignore them is a mistake.

Three scenarios are envisioned as plausible future ways in which LCI data might be collected, managed, assessed, and used. The scenarios serve as the basis of discussion about what each might imply for LCI data along the dimensions of utility, accessibility, and composability. New knowledge management technologies, combined with societal trends in the way that knowledge is being created and managed, are likely to change our ideas about what constitutes LCA data, and these changes likely will pose significant challenges to LCA database providers. The provider will be expected to create LCA knowledge management frameworks in which data are more distributed, more mobile, more democratic, and more standardized, and yet providers will also be expected to make sure the data continue to be interoperable between applications and platforms.

5.7 INTEGRATION

A careful examination of existing guidance from dozens of regional and national-level references are brought to focus for analysis process. However, topics are not to stand alone in how they influence the primary objective of the document. One element of this integration encompasses all the aspects of the current practices. A systematic treatment of data from the earliest stages of data sourcing and collection

60   Life Cycle Assessment

through inclusion of reviewed data sets into databases, maintaining a clear view of the requirement of those databases is incredibly important to provide the best support of database users and strongly recommended by the guidance principles. Data sourcing and data collection are the starting points of any of the unit processes and aggregated process data sets or any of the LCA databases. The importance of data sourcing and data collection is often underestimated, and the ISO standard on product LCA does not address it sufficiently. Hence, UNEP/SETAC published the Shonan Guidance Principles document to explain the principle of raw data collection for LCA, which is understood as data that has not yet been put into relation to LCI process data sets. Starting at this early point of helps ensure the resulting LCA data set will have the desired quality and extent of documentation. Data collection is defined as the process of gathering data for specific purposes. Data collection has the aim to deliver data needed for one or several specific unit process data sets both the input and output flows and metadata that describes the process. A broad range of data collection methods exist, ranging from direct on-location primary measurements to various secondary estimation techniques. Some aspects of good practices of data collection procedure are given as well. The identification of good practice, wherever it is possible to do so, helps the consistency and interchangeability of data sets that the guidance document strives to provide. However, in some areas, there may not be a single good practice, or experts may not have been able to reach consensus. Data collection is intricately linked to unit process development. Life cycle inventory unit process development procedures of specific data and supplement information for data documentation are required, and the ensuing data collection effort tries to provide this information. In parallel with the collection of the raw data, there needs to be proper documentation, which is able to later derive the required documentation at the next steps of unit process and aggregated data. Data collection is also linked to validation and quality assurance. The validation process starts from the data as they are used in the process model. Results of the validation process may lead to the conclusion that further data are needed or that the data used are insufficient. Validation at the data set level serves to ensure that the model represents the actual process.

Using ISO standards as a starting point, the guidance documents make a key distinction between a "unit process data set" and an "aggregated process data set." The Shonan Guidance Principles provide recommendations at a global level regarding the process of converting raw data into a unit process data set, including the phases of goal and scope definition as applicable to the intended purpose of the data set development, data set generation, validation verification, and documentation. In principle, the creation of a unit process data set should be guided by the intended application specified in the goal and scope phase of the data development activity. It is recommended to keep the content of the unit process data set flexible so that it can be used in different application contexts. In particular, the multifunctional data set might be provided in its unallocated form, which allows the end user to apply either allocation or system expansion as is appropriate for the decision context.

There are good reasons to provide data sets on the unit process level. First, unit process data provides maximum transparency, allowing the user of the database

Guidance for Life Cycle Inventory

to understand which unit process are used in the life of given reference flow and how these unit processes are linked. Second, you need process data to make the database flexible and adaptable in the sense that unit processes in a specific LCI life cycle inventory can better reflect the situation to be assessed. Third, unit process data can improve the interpretation of the life cycle studies because of the high resolution of the unit. Process-based assessment allows a user to identify the key unit processes to perform sensitivity analysis by varying methodological and other assumptions, as well as parameters, inputs, and outputs.

The credibility of an LCA database very much depends on the quality of the raw data used and the unit process data sets developed from those data. The creation of unit process data sets, as well as the modeling of aggregated process data sets, requires technical, scientific, engineering, and economic knowledge, as well as familiarity with LCA methodology. It is recommended that the independent verification conducted on unit process data sets provides a stand-alone data set in an LCI database, and those unit process data sets are used to generate aggregated process data sets along with the product system and the model used. There are several reasons to aggregate data sets. First, when answering questions typically addressed by LCA, it is often more convenient to work with the aggregated process data sets (cradle-to-gate, cradle-to-grave) in a number of LCA software systems and in simplified tools because their use can reduce calculation time and memory requirement. Furthermore, from the user perspective, it can be beneficial to work with aggregated or even LCI system-level data sets if the user does not have the technical or engineering ability to model a complex process chain, such as a steel plant or refinery. Finally, the aggregation of data sets may be required for confidentiality reasons. Confidentiality may be ensured by different levels of aggregation by establishing an industry average, by aggregating some selected unit process and data sets along the supply chain, or by aggregating unit process data sets with selected input being followed from the cradle. For these cases, an aggregated, reviewed data set with comprehensive documentation can be an appropriate choice. Data sets from databases can be used in different modeling approaches like attributional, consequential, and decisional. Consistency is key to allow these changes to be made by users. Different approaches exist to model product system. These approaches can be the basis for generating aggregated cradle-to-gate and cradle-to-grave process data sets. The modeling approaches are different, and one approach cannot be recommended as the general best approach. It is advisable that user make the decision about the modeling approach by looking at the explicit decision context of their LCA study. It is recommended that the aggregate process data sets be modeled as consistently as necessary and that any inconsistency be documented when relevant. The data set provider must be clear about the modeling approach used when creating aggregated process data sets. Next to consistency and drawing on good documentation, the accuracy of the data sets that will be combined into the life cycle model deserves special attention. The technological, geographic, and temporal representativeness determine whether the modeled life cycle is sufficiently descriptive of the system it is meant to represent. Data sets of sufficient representativeness are recommended.

6 Application of Life Cycle Assessment

6.1 LIFE CYCLE THINKING: POLICY MAKERS

Government develops environmental policy while negotiating with all stakeholders and NGOs for volunteer agreements with industry, keeps considering the life cycle thinking. Measuring potential life cycle impact of decisions can help government programs and prioritize these programs based on life cycle information. Policies should be more consistent among consumers, producers, material suppliers, retailers, and waste managers. Subsidies purchase product and service which are environmental preferable and reduce the impact. Government operation has an environment and support regional and global market for preferable products and services, which promotes pricing of the products and service to accurately reflect the cost of environmental degradation and impact at the life cycle stages. Such price signals can send messages to consumers and provide incentives for businesses to continuously improve the environmental and social performance of products or services across their life cycles—for instance, introduction of take-back systems to establish a recycling based CE. Thinking in terms of life cycles, businesses recognize that each choice sets the stage for not only how the product will look and function but also how it will impact the environment and the community as it is manufactured, reuses and recycles. Each product characteristic is determined when the product is designed and will impact the environment differently.

With the life cycle information, companies can calculate the full life cycle cost of the goods they purchase. This includes the point of purchase price as well as the cost of transporting, storing installing, cleaning, operating, repairing, and eventually discarding those goods, which is also known as the total cost of owning that product. So, a product design with better environmental, social, and economic performance across its life cycle may have benefited that the company can communicate to its customers. Some business elective use product declarations are having beneficial level to market and more environmental and social attributes to their customers. There are international standards for these business-to-business communications, also called environmental product declarations. Each declaration must be based on a life cycle study and tell the business customer about the life cycle and more environmental impacts of the components of the product being purchased. Life cycle thinking that influences a product design, strategic planning, and procurement and sales helps businesses promote their image and the value of their brands. Businesses can avoid criticism and participate in issue-based conferences to update oneself. Finding a new way of marketing and sales

DOI: 10.1201/9781003206750-6

64 Life Cycle Assessment

department is to communicate and interact with customers. Some 50 percent of business say they are interested in learning about sustainability. This means a company can promote its product and services by talking about its social and environmental attributes. By sharing life cycle information with suppliers, customers, and waste handlers to identify risk and opportunity for the improvement, the risk might relate to the environment for one's health safety and finance, while opportunity could include growing market share, brand image, effective use of materials, and innovation. Together businesses can find new ways to improve output while optimizing their use of time, money, labor, and materials to improve environmental impact throughout product or service life cycles.

Industry and market interest in environmental information on products that is credible, unbiased, verifiable, and covers the entire life cycle is growing rapidly. The information should cover the product life cycle from acquiring raw materials to recycling those materials when the product is no longer in use. Through environmental product declarations (EPDs) meant to provide this type of information in business-to-business communication, business can promote green procurement in private and public sectors companies. Global manufacturers' use of EPDs to communicate their products' environmental performance with advanced technology for utility helps industry and customers.

LCT can be put into practice in many ways involving a number of different tools and company reports on environmental and social issues, which helps individual citizens bring LCT into purchasing decisions. Governments can take up a life cycle approach to policymaking by evolving a wide range of stakeholders such as product panel life cycle modeling, and new policy approach, in private sector company's engineers, and designers apply life cycle thinking when designing product and service via studies based on life cycle assessment.

Experts from the industry, government, and R&D organizations agree that making a life cycle approach part of the way an organization or person designs products, develops services, makes policies, and decides what to consume and what not to consume will help to halt and possibly reverse some of the impact reduction on the communities and the environments. It certainly helps to solve some environmental problems, but it can also help us find *sustainable* ways to tackle some of them effectively. The life cycle approach is a holistic way to promote fruitful and economic development while respecting the natural environment and its resources. The government and prominent global multinational corporations currently use LCT, and future planning demonstrates that the economic, environmental, and social benefits are tangible.

6.2 ATTRIBUTIONAL LIFE CYCLE ASSESSMENT

In defining the scope of attributional LCA, the goal must be clearly understood and defined. Before a goal definition and attributional LCA is set, the decision and stakeholder situation in which the performer of attributional LCA resides must be clearly understood. The goal and scope definition phase in life cycle assessment when applied to attributional life cycle assessment (ALCA) methodology is important

Application of Life Cycle Assessment

because attributional LCA methodology is used by many different stakeholders. To respect the nature of the different stakeholders, it is important to understand their roles in relation to the life cycle approach before interpreting aspects of the goal and scope. LCAs are done in time frames ranging from several days to several years. Therefore the following aspects are important and must be addressed unambiguously according to ISO 14040-2006 and ISO 14044-2006. One of the main aims of ISO is to reduce misinterpretation and miscommunication and to increase probability of detecting flaws in the assessment, results, and interpretation and to iteratively remove these. Therefore, special attention and rule sets are applied to results, which are intended to be used in comparative assertions intended to be disclosed to the public. So, it shall be unambiguously stated if and how the results relate to the comparisons to alternative systems and if this is intended to be made public.

Handbook of International Life Cycle Data System (ILCD) has been published. The life cycle data network as well as the Product Environmental Footprint (PEF) initiative are core activities that have influenced the LCA landscape over the last few years. Today most LCA stakeholders, producers, and consumers of LCA information can be sorted across groups such as industry and the private sector; academia and education; and NGOs. The various interests and needs developed semiquantitative estimates of the magnitude of LCA work performed and published. Academia has cognitive interests, models development, is interested in basic science, and is calling for transparency of public data. The classical LCA approach was without crucial decision aspects. Industry has a solution. Engineering credibility of the results for use in product optimization and decision support is in the foreground. The approach is to be integrated into daily operation with transparent workflows defined. Since most of the performed LCA work is not publicly shared, most results contain sensitive information and intellectual property that could give competitive advantage to somebody, but it is on demand or selectively shared; it is not easy to determine the absolute number of performed LCAs. However, the chance that the vast majority of all LCAs ever undertaken are "attributional" is highly probable. Once the different stakeholder positions, needs, and responsibilities are understood, the goal of the work is clearly defined; then the scope of the work and focus need to be defined and described, that is, the technology or system under study; and then the standard needs to be applied, and the attributional methodology option applied. The word *attribution* is used to describe and explain the causes of behavior and events. In the case of LCA, attributional methodology describes and explains the causations of processes and process chains. The beauty of attributional LCA coping with probable future effects is that it is based on a defined range of suitable technical and market parameters in certain defined and documented cases. Hence, attributional LCA methodology can be both retrospectively and prospectively applied.

6.3 CONSEQUENTIAL LIFE CYCLE ASSESSMENT

When LCA first originated as an environmental management tool, it was used to assess single products. As the methodology developed throughout the 1990s developers recognized the need to provide a sense of importance and influence of the possible consequence of future development and technology or changes to supply chain. It was also seen as being useful in supporting large scale decision for the organization. The rise of this alternative perspective on LCA application was inspired by many research institutes. LCA practitioners began to realize that the direction of the current development of LCA modeling was not always open to identifying all consequences. The notion behind this realization was that certain decisions could result in impacts outside the defined system, and as such, should be factored into decision-making processes. This approach is to identify study boundaries to encompass consequences of an action or decision known as consequential LCA (CLCA) modeling. This term differentiates the approach from the more accountancy-oriented approach, which became known as ALCA modeling. To incorporate consequences, CLCA modeling includes additional economic data like marginal production cost, electricity of supply and demand, and so forth. Therefore, it is more conceptually rich. As for all modeling, the results are extremely sensitive to the assumptions that are made. Keeping track of all exemptions is crucial for transparency and should be clearly identified in the final assessment report.

Many attempts have been made to describe when several types of LCA are appropriate. As with consequential LCA and attributional LCA, similar distinctions have been made between others using different terms to denote types of LCA, such as "descriptive" versus "change-oriented" and "marginal" versus "market oriented." Briefly, ALCA focuses on describing the environmentally relevant impacts of the activity that contributes to a specific property of a product or process, while consequential assessment describes how environmentally relevant impacts will, or could, change in response to the studied action or decision. The difference between attributional and consequential LCA are the result of the choices made in the goal and scope definition phase of the general LCA process.

It is argued that consequential LCA should be used for decision-making, but not when the difference between consequential and attributional LCA result is small, and not when uncertainty in the consequential modeling outweigh the insights gained from it. When no decision is at hand, attributional LCA should be used because it is more universally applied method and because modeling consequences of decision is pointless when no decision is it end at hand. Similar arguments have been presented by other authors. Although commonly found in practice, neither attributional nor consequential LCA are specified in ISO standards. More importantly, there is no standardized guidance on selecting an attributional or a consequential LCA approach to properly support goal of the study. This aspect of the goal is not well addressed at the methodological or practical level, despite its relevance. Even though the correct formulation of a question is central in every evaluation, its importance continues to be neglected. There is a lack of depth to this important aspect as the origin of this dispute between consequential LCA and other types of LCA and, consequently, the lack of clarity about the context in which CLCA could be applied. In response to the gap, method developers have provided various guidance documents to users on how to approach CLCA.

Application of Life Cycle Assessment 67

Consequential LCA modeling has been adopted by some LCA practitioner and academia for the analysis of product system, answering questions on what could be the result of production or consumption decisions. It is valid in assessing the environmental consequences of the individual decision or rules. Attributional LCA, a more static, technical descriptive analysis, is valid for identifying connection between system and potential environmental impacts. Both ALCA and CLCA have utility for use in decision-making, as well as limitations. The main difference consists in how boundaries are defined, which stems from a clear unambiguous definition of the goal of the study. How to better link questions and models is an important field of research, not only for CLCA, but for all LCA approaches. As a guideline for individual LCA studies, it is important to emphasize how the question is framed, clear identification of the problem to be addressed, what the derived questions are, what the technological options are, what the scale of the expected changes is, what the timeframe of the questions is, if all things being equal assumptions will hold, whether the system being analyzed is replacing another system at a small scale, and whether the technology used in the new system is expected to extend to many more application on a larger scale. Model choices are extremely sensitive to assumptions and so forth, with the risk that inadequate assumptions or other errors significantly affect the final LCA results. To reduce this risk, it is important to ensure that the various consequences can be explained using credible arguments. The distinction between attributional and consequential LCA is one example of how choices in the goal and scope definition of an LCA influence methodological and data choices for LCI and LCIA phases.

6.4   INTEGRATION AND HARMONIZATION

LCA focuses on the environmental impact of a product or service. When choosing among various alternates the final decision is made by combining the result of LCA with other aspects, including cost and social implications, economic performance, and technical feasibility. These aspects are evaluated with other supplementary analysis tools such as LCC and SLCA, which link these environmental impacts to the system function that facilitates the entire life cycle of a product or service from cradle to grave. It is essential to account for the entirety of the product's life cycle activities to avoid suggesting local environmental improvements that effectively export pollution to other parts of the life cycle. These life cycle activities take place upstream from the business in question as well as downstream including, for example, the type of material that needs to be extracted, the electricity required during the use days, or the disposal required in the waste management.

LCA provides information that can be used by the government, businesses, and other decision makers. LCA is an iterative tool that helps to integrate with distinct aspects of life cycle assessment like LCC, SLCA, and OLCA. Even ELCA helps to trace the footprint of both carbon and water. In general action and policy are directly influenced by overarching concepts and procedural environmental methods. Such procedural tools include equal leveling, which levels have set up product as service within specific functional category friendly and environmental

68   Life Cycle Assessment

audit which assess the environmental performance of an individual business and provide follow up suggestion an environmental impact assessment. Specifically, LCSA is a deeper integration among the various aspects, namely, environmental, social, and economic, regarding their mutual relationship and reciprocal effect. An overall assessment that is the direct application of LCA with some ELCA, plus SLCA and LCC fails to provide a result that is more than the sum of its parts. To integrate different aspects of LCSA and in order to fill the gap between modeling and reality that reduces the uncertainty inherent to the modeling activity, a multi-method approach is widely regarded as being needed. From the beginning of LCSA application the interesting transdisciplinary nature of the subject was recognized as requiring an integration of methods and models of environment, economic, and social issues and their impacts. Given is the issue of selection, sharing, and availability of these models and a proper matching between models, integrating to address all the parameters of sustainability of a product. In a process within the framework of growing CE, LCSA should also be able to adapt to include tools able to model engulfing industrial symbiosis, circular material flow analysis, and resource scarcity. Many analytical approaches have been recently explored as opportunities to improve the traditional LCSA.

6.5 INDUSTRIAL UNIT

The application of LCA in industry or enterprises can be classified into five main purposes:

1. Decision support in product and process development.
2. Marketing point of view.
3. Development and selection of indicators used in monitoring environmental performance of a product's plans.
4. Selection of supplier our subcontractors.
5. Static planning.

LCA application within industry may well serve more than one purpose, and often the same LCA can be used for different purposes within the company. Product development is often combined with marketing efforts, so LCA can be used to study an industry both internally and externally. Furthermore, as experience with using LCA grows in an enterprise, one application can trigger another insight. Gains from LCA studies of products and performance can lead to decisions about selection of suppliers and strategic goal setting. LCA is often used during product development and for identifying environmental hot spots of a product and process either within organizations or in a supply chain.

6.6 SMALL AND MEDIUM-SIZED ENTERPRISES

Small and medium-sized enterprises (SMEs) can use LCA for the same reasons large companies use LCA. SMEs have lagged large companies in their

Application of Life Cycle Assessment

implementation of LCA. The major reason is thought to be the cost of an LCA study, the need of changes in workplace routines, perceived complexity of the LCA methodology, and shortage of qualified personnel to carry out an LCA. Few SMEs revealed that a downside of LCA is that it becomes comprehensive and too complex to be easily understood, leaving an impression in some companies of LCA as a black box. Exclusive collaboration with the experienced LCA practitioner expert was found to resolve this problem in some of the cases. Similarly, according to a comprehensive literature review, it is reported that major barriers for implementation of sustainability management tools such as LCA by SMEs include the following: lack of awareness of sustainability issues, absence of perceived benefits, lack of knowledge and expertise on sustainability issues, lack of trained manpower and financial resources, insufficient external drivers and incentives, and complexity of tool and its adaptation and interpretation. While the use of LCA by SMEs was considered marginal, it consistently become increasingly common in developed economy, service provided by LCA practitioners. This may be due to the increased legislative focus on environmental performance and potential market benefits from having an environmentally friendly profile.

6.7 CORPORATE LEVEL

The user will see in the product document that monitored environmental performance at the corporate level is today often limited to a few selected impact categories, typically footprint indicators like carbon and water. This situation may change in the future together with the development of guidelines of the organizational environmental footprint of at the corporate level. Industries are using LCA for setting strategic objectives. Currently, global market for multinational corporations is organizing all stakeholders to implement all relevant green initiatives to have a competitive edge in response to consumer sensibilities regarding global environmental concerns.

If green and sustainable development is a big challenge to the industry, it is also an opportunity for the corporate world as they have a smart and young innovative workforce with financial strength and can take radical shifts in their approach. Most corporate offices are developing their own long green path towards carbon neutrality.

6.8 CONSUMER PERSPECTIVE

LCA results can also serve as a decision support for individuals, be it in the capacity of a citizen or a consumer. In many cases these decisions lead to the private consumption of goods and services. Consumers are knowingly or unknowingly exposed onto LCA results or conclusions drawn from LCA results through consumer information from the producers' packaging and media reporting of academic findings. They hold some power through their influence in the market of products. Consumer decisions that may be supported by an LCA can range from choosing the product with the lowest environmental impact from a group of related products. The green space is favorable for consumer involvement, largely because environmental impacts, like climate change, are visible globally, and the market is turning green, as consumers are aware of the common advantages of environmental-friendly products.

7 Climate Change and Life Cycle Assessment

7.1 ON THE HORIZON

The interaction between industry and the natural environment is well known on the climate change and other environmental impacts. Most of the industrial manufacturing have been identified and agreed very widely to reduce emissions of various pollutants. It is increased pressure on various policy makers of governments and industrial houses. Climate change is on the horizon, and everybody feels its heat in several ways. GHG emissions fuel climate change and the mechanism has been proven scientifically. The Paris Agreement is a legally binding international treaty on climate change. It was adopted by 196 parties (countries) at COP 21 in Paris, on 12 December 2015 and entered into force on 4 November 2016. Its goal is to limit global warming to well below 2°C, preferably to 1.5°C, compared to preindustrial levels. To achieve this long-term temperature goal, countries aim to reach global peaking of GHG emissions as soon as possible to achieve a climate neutral world by mid-century. The Paris Agreement is a landmark in the multilateral climate change process because, for the first time, a binding agreement brings all nations into a common cause to undertake ambitious efforts to combat climate change and adapt to its effects.

Now this is more comprehensive than ever before: a global climate deal agreeing to a long-term goal of limiting increasing the global average temperature to well below 2°C, which means that countries need to scale up their efforts and actions to reduce the emissions. It will bring great challenges for industries of different sectors as those consider producing GHG. The existence of environmental regulations has been a considerable influence on some of the companies. The demand for renewal ecological resources and the service it provides is now equivalent to that of more than 1.5 times of Earth's resources. In the cement and construction industries, LCA is very useful to find out various paths to reduce GHG emissions, which ultimately would improve the climate condition. Therefore, the renewable energy fuels have become so important for replacement of non-renewal fuels, since it takes millions of years from dead plants to transform into coal and using them as one of the major sources of energy is not sustainable in the long run. The building and construction industries are responsible for 39 percent of carbon emissions globally. Eleven percent from construction materials is also known as embodied carbon. The cement industry is also responsible for producing GHG emissions to the tune of 6 percent of total GHG produced in the world. In view of the life cycle study in both cement and construction industry, it will be helpful to

DOI: 10.1201/9781003206750-7

72　　　　　　　　　　　　　　　　　　　　　　　　　Life Cycle Assessment

understand how to use alternate raw materials and fuels to reduce CO_2 to mitigate climate change.

7.2　ENVIRONMENTAL MECHANISM

In principle, the energy reaching the Earth's atmosphere from solar radiation and leaving it again via reflection and infrared radiation is in balance, creating a stable temperature regime in our atmosphere. The sunlight reaching the Earth's atmosphere, one fraction less than 28 percent, is directly reflected into space by air molecules, clouds, and the surface of the Earth, particularly ocean and icy regions such as the Arctic and Antarctic. This effect is called "albedo." The remainder is absorbed in the atmosphere by greenhouse gases GHG (21 percent) and the Earth's surface (50 percent). The latter heats up the planetary surface and is released back into the atmosphere as infrared radiation (black body radiation) with a longer wavelength than the absorbed radiation. This infrared radiation is partially absorbed by GHGs and therefore kept in the atmosphere instead of being released into space, explaining why the temperature of the atmosphere increases with its content of GHGs. LCA studies provide intensity of the impact of GWP and find out alternative methods for the reduction of GWP especially in the cement and construction industries.

The IPCC 2014 defines climate change as "a change in the state of climate that can be identified using statistical test by changes in the mean and/or the variability of its properties, and that persists for an extended period, typically decades add longer." The IPCC observed an acceleration of the rise in planetary surface temperature in the last five to six decades, with the highest rates at the very northern latitudes of the Arctic. Ocean temperatures are also on the rise down to a depth of at least 3000 meters and have so far absorbed most of the heat trapped in the atmosphere.

7.3　REDUCTION MEASURE OF GHG

Heat waves' variation of hydrological system affects both quantity and quality of water resources. It has negative impact of climate change on crop yields. Due to its impacts, there are possibilities of shifting of geographic ranges, seasonal activities, migration patterns, and species interaction including biodiversity by many territorial freshwater and marine species-changes in the infectious disease vectors. Mitigating global climate change requires not only government action but also cooperation from industries as well as consumers. The findings of a few studies suggested that more attention needs to be given to the social and psychological motivation as to why individuals encounter barriers to climate change mitigation in their personal commitment, even when professing anxiety over the future of climatic conditions. The climate change mitigation mechanisms and their impact on sustainable development are key factors for consideration. Climate change mitigation architects have different impact categories for different groups of countries. Therefore, sustainability assessment is performed by

Climate Change and Life Cycle Assessment

different group of countries. It is essential for all developing and emerging economy countries because a delicate balance is required for development projects and taking mitigating measures for climate change. It is a very challenging situation for developing countries, hence financial aid from developed nation becomes pivotal. COP26 at Glasgow has suggested solution to deal with climate change globally. But COP26 did produce new "building blocks" to advance implementation of the Paris Agreement through actions that can get the world on a more sustainable, low-carbon pathway forward.

The cost of GHG emission mitigation has become more complex recently over the existence of economic and environmental double dividends that have been added. The existence of negative cost potential industrialized countries may reduce their cost by meeting carbon constraints if they penalize fuel not only based on their carbon intensity but also on the basis of their import and export. It has been summarized by selective studies of the potential and cost of carbon emission mitigation strategy in the post plan economy. The long-term mission and their mitigation in a household of high economic and energy demand growth scenario in which technological change unfolds in alternate path-dependent directions of the climate change mitigation assessment for developing country with a special emphasis on economic studies. It was observed that the GHG emission from developing countries certainly will increase in the future due to economic development needs.

There is a however a large and cheap potential for emission reduction connected to efficiency improvement in industrial production in general energy efficiency improvement in the countries. The implementation of GHG mitigation strategy is entirely related to the general national economic development policies. The macroeconomic impact of implementing climate change mitigation strategies should be assessed. But it is observed that the project implementation and economic welfare improvement in some cases can be achieved simultaneously, on a logical basis for macroeconomic assessment and the establishment of baseline scenarios. Specific planning contexts of developing countries need research and financial assistance to identify the best price difference in approach in bottom-up CO_2 emission reduction costing for the energy sector for developing countries.

7.4 CARBON SEQUESTRATION

Carbon sequestration is an important technology for the maintenance of optimum CO_2 levels in the atmosphere. It is an important factor for mitigation of climate change. Carbon sequestration has been a sensitive analysis for its cost and the relative importance of sequestration technology is the long-term carbon management framework and suggested that carbon recovery with geological sequestration could be included among the available carbon abatement. The carbon transport and storage cost exemption have been explored, particularly the issue of how to ensure adequate long-term monitoring and maintenance of the carbon sequestration sites. The bonding mechanism the symmetry of sequestration/sequestration process at a micro level end of its consequences at a macro level taking explicitly

74 Life Cycle Assessment

into account the temporarily of sequestration. It showed that with this exemption must be permanent although it has received relatively little attention of ocean and geographical locations for sequestration. It is a potential method of combating climate change in component in comparison to energy reduction measure. The development of carbon free energy technologies sequestration of carbon dioxide in geologic or sparing oil well/sinks are having enormous potential. But there are concern about the possible maintenance cost.

7.5 CARBON CAPTURE THROUGH ALGAE

Increasing concentration of greenhouse gas is a matter of great environmental concern. Many attempts have been made to recover carbon dioxide from the atmosphere using physical and chemical treatments. In a biological approach, microalgae appear more photosynthetically efficient than terrestrial plants and are efficient carbon dioxide fixers. Once it was known that microalgae have a potential to consume more carbon dioxide than the atmospheric level, microalgae started being used as biological scrubbers to mitigate thermal power and cement plant stacks gases. Microalgae are of great interest because of their rapid growth rate and tolerance to varying environmental conditions like kiln exit gas. The carbon fixed by the microalgae is incorporated into energy rich biomass, which is widely used as an excellent source of lipids, cofiring fuel, and as animal feed. Kiln stack gas contains 12 to 20 percent carbon dioxide and contains some of the combustible products such as NOx and SOx, which can be effectively used as nutrients by microalgae and thus a high purity of carbon dioxide is not required for the growth of microalgae. Therefore, direct injection of flue gas into carbon dioxide sequestration systems can reduce the cost of separation of carbon dioxide from the flue gas. Several species of algae have been tested for carbon dioxide sequestration.

The cement manufacturing sector is under close environmental scrutiny these days because of large volumes of carbon dioxide emitted from kiln stacks. Currently there are no emission limits on carbon dioxide emission in cement plants due to calcination and combustion in pyro processing. This method has its limitation for the reduction of CO_2 emissions in view of high carbon dioxide level from cement sector. There is no other way than to capture and storage (CCS) is the only possible option for tangible carbon dioxide abatement. Cement sector looks forward for CCS measures for potential carbon dioxide mitigation. Till date no concrete solution of CO_2 capture from kill in stack is economical feasible through several CCS studies. Besides technical aspects, the economic framework will be decisive for application of carbon capture in the cement plant. In fact, post-combustion capture, an end-of-pipe measure that would not require any basic modification in the pyro processing of clinker production, has some advantages.

7.6 OZONE FORMATION

The halogen compounds in the stratosphere mostly originate from very stable industrial halocarbon gases used as solvent or refrigerant the dechlorinated CFC or

Climate Change and Life Cycle Assessment

Freon, the brominated halons. Groups of anthropogenic ozone depleting substances (ODS) are bromochloromethanes (BCM), CFC, carbon tetrachloride, hydrobromo-fluorocarbon (HBFCs), hydrochlorofluorocarbons (HCFCs), tetrachloromethane, 1,1,1-trichloroethane, methyl bromide, methyl chloride, and halons. The main uses of ODS during the last century were fire extinguishing systems (halon), plastic foams, propellant gas in spray cans, fumigation and pesticides (methyl bromide), metered-dose inhalers (MDIs), refrigeration and air conditioning, and solvent decreasing. Natural ozone depleting substance are CH_4, N_2O, H_2O, and halogenated substances with sufficient stability and/or release rates to allow them to reach the stratosphere. All ozone-depleting substances have two common characteristics: chemically, they are very stable in lower atmospheres and also capable of releasing chloride and bromide under UV radiation. The phasing out of production and use of substances of concern has been successfully enforced under the Montreal protocol, which was signed in 1987 and led to the phasing out of consumption and production of ODS by 1996 in developed countries and by 2010 in developing countries. If it is continuously respected, this effort should lead to the cessation of the appearance of the ozone hole around 2070. The delay exists because we are still emitting decreasing amounts of relevant substances, mostly during the end-of-the life treatment of old refrigeration and air conditioning systems and they are very persistent and may take decades to reach the pole. When significant emissions are dominating, impacts of ODS are absorbed in LCIs or LCA results. Nowadays, the data originate from references before the phase out and hence it is rarity due to absolute data unless the end-of-life treatment of old refrigeration and air conditioning system are an important component of the LCA studies.

The impact category appears under different categories in LCIA methods. One of them is photochemical ozone formation under several different names but in essence they all address the impact from ozone and other reactive oxygen compounds formed as a secondary contaminant in the tropospheric by the oxidation of primary contaminants like volatile organic compounds are carbon monoxide in the presence of nitrogen oxides under the influence of light. NO_x is a joint name for nitrogen monoxide and nitrogen dioxide. The photochemical formation of ozone and other reactive oxygen compounds in the troposphere from emissions of VOC and NO_x follows a complex reaction that depends on the nature of specific organic compounds emitted. Reduction of NO_x from thermal power stations, steel plants, cement plants, and other chemical industries is required.

Ozone Version 43 is a highly reactive and unstable molecule consisting of three oxygen atoms and forms a bluish gas at normal ambient temperature. This molecule is present in lower atmospheric layer tropospheric ozone sequence of photochemical ozone formation an enlarged concentration about 8 PPMV also in higher altitude between 15 and 40 kilometers above the ground stratospheric ozone. Tropospheric ground level ozone a pollutant does too many harmful effects there on human animal plants and materials. Hence, how well is a component of stratospheric atmosphere layer it is vital to life on planet earth due to its capacity to absorb energy rich UV radiation thus preventing destructive amounts of it from reaching life on planet surface. Status very causal depletion refers to the declining concentration

76   Life Cycle Assessment

of stratospheric 1970s which are observed in various ways is the ozone depletion area are ozone hole an ambiguous term often used in public clear referring to an area of critically lower stratospheric ozone. ozone holes have been observed over the Antarctic since early 1980. A general decline of several percentage points per decade in ozone concentration has been observed. Autumn concentration is considered as critically low when the value of integrated ozone column falls below 220 drop some units in normal value being about 300 Dobson units.

7.7 EUTROPHICATION

Nutrients occur naturally in the environment, where they are a fundamental precondition for the existence of life. The species composition and productivity of different ecosystems reflect the availability of nutrients, and natural differences in the availability of nitrogen and phosphorus are thus one of the reasons for the existing multiplicity of species and of different types of ecosystems. These are dynamic and if they are affected by changes in the availability of nutrients they simply adapt to a new balance with their surroundings. Originally, eutrophication of aquatic environments, such as rivers or lakes, described its eutrophic character, meaning poor conditions and low oxygen levels for supporting life. Eutrophication describes the enrichment of the aquatic environment with nutrients that increases salts leading to an increased biomass production of planktonic algae, gelatinous zooplankton, and higher aquatic plants, which results in the degradation of water quality.

7.8 ECOTOXICITY

Ecotoxicity is not the only parameter that determines the potential impact effect of a chemical in the environment, as it must quickly enter a potential target organism. For example, a substance may be very toxic but never reaches any organism due to its short lifetime in the environment due to rapid degradation or because it is not sufficiently mobile to be transported to its target organism and ends up bound to soil or buried in sediment, in which case it contributes little to the ecotoxic impacts. On the other hand, another substance may not be very toxic, but if it is emitted in large quantities over prolonged periods of time or has a strong environmental persistence, it may still cause an ecotoxic impact. Chemical emissions into the environment will affect terrestrial, freshwater, marine, and aerial flying and gliding animals' ecosystems depending on the environmental condition of the place and time of emission and the characteristics of the substance emitted. They can affect the natural organism in many ways, causing increased mortality, reduce mobility, reduced growth or reproduction rate, mutation, behavioral changes, changes in biomass or photosynthesis, activity, and so forth. The ecosystem is typically considered a midpoint indicator in LCA, as no distinction between the severity of observed effects is made. The method for toxic impact assessment of chemicals in the framework of LCA must be able to cover the very

Climate Change and Life Cycle Assessment

large number of potentially toxic substances in the inventory in terms of available characterization factors.

7.9 HUMAN TOXICITY

The human toxicity impact category has several things in common with other forms of toxicity impact, like main emissions and sources, modeling principles, model structure—even some of the models used in the characterization are identical between the human toxicity and ecotoxicity impact categories. Notably the fate model (transfer of chemicals from environment into the food and water ingested by humans) used is the same in LCIA method using mechanistic characterizes in modeling, which is most existing methods. Therefore, only those parts that are specific for human toxicity and different from ecotoxicity are required to understand the main underlying principle. Human toxicity in LCA is based on the same driving factors as in ecotoxicity: emitted quantity determined in the LCI, mobility, persistence, exposure pattern. Human toxicity is considered by the four characterization factors. The respective mechanisms and parameters are certainly different and specific for human toxicity, notably for exposure and modeling, where there are many factors, such as dietary habits, that influence human exposure patterns. Chemical exposure of humans can result from emission into the environment that will occur during production, use, or end-of-life treatment, thus affecting workers and consumers.

7.10 ABIOTIC RESOURCES

Natural resources constitute the material foundation of our society and economies and, paraphrasing the definition of sustainability by United Nations Commissions on Environment and Development (the Brundtland Commission), they are as such fundamental for our abilities to fulfill our needs as well as us for future generations to fulfill their own needs. We must ensure that future resource availability is possible compared to the current generation's situation. We must consider the future availability of all resources that we know and dispose of today. The definition of natural resources has an anthropocentric starting point. What humans need from nature to sustain their livelihood and activity is a resource. For context of LCA, the natural resources are those elements that are extracted from earth for use. They comprise both abiotic resources such as fossil fuels and mineral ores and biotic resources such as wood and fish. They have a functional value in society. Although water and land are also resources, their use causes direct impact on the environment. In this respect they differ from the other resources, and they are therefore treated as an individual impact category and described as separate impacts.

Currently, the resource use impact category covers mostly fossil fuel minerals and metals. In terms of future availability of a resource the issue is not current extraction and use of resources per se but depletion or dissipation of the resources. Like the use of land, the use of resources can be viewed from an occupation perspective and transformation perspective. While a resource is used in a way for

78 Life Cycle Assessment

one purpose, it is not available for other purpose, and there is thus a competitive situation. When resources are used in a way that caters to their easy reuse at the end of the product life, they are still occupied and not immediately available to others for use, but they are in principle available to future use for other purposes.

7.11 AFFORESTATION

One strategy for mitigating the increase in the atmospheric carbon dioxide is to expand the size of terrestrial carbon sinks, particularly forests expansion, by planting of trees for afforestation projects. The framework of the convention on climate change includes many provisions for forest and land use as carbon sequestration projects. This activity in the signatories overall GHG mitigation plans even the impartial analysis have in assessing the carbon offset benefit of the project. The potential for developing synergies between climate change mitigation and adaptation has become a recent focus of both climate research and policies. There are also increasing calls for research to define the optimal mix of mitigation and adaptation. The diagrammatic representation of climate change adaptation and mitigation is important in conceptualizing the problem. In identifying importance feedbacks and communicating between disciplines with a more refined distance in between adaptation and mitigation. It is found that emphasis on issue-based solution plays more on mitigation strategy then adaptation and responsibilities are suggested for dealing with climate change. Most of the analysis has focused on the case, where the actions available to society are just mitigation of emission.

7.12 LAND USE

Land use refers to anthropogenic activity in each soil area. Examples of land use are agriculture and forestry production, urban settlement, and mineral extraction. The land use type in a specific area can be identified by physical covers of its surface, for example, any crop grown in the open field. In some case like orchids under greenhouse, artificial surface with infrastructure is expression of human settlement and open pits are sign of one of all extraction. There is a direct link between land use and land cover, which is used to analyze land use dynamics and landscape change patterns.

Characterization of land use in LCA has been extensively debated over the last few decades but is far from being settled, because the first operational methods have only been available since 2010. Until then, land use was only an inventory flow counted in units of surface occupied and time of occupation (m^2 and years) and surface transformed (m^2), without any associated impact. The main reason for this development is that land-use-related impacts rely on spatial and temporal conditions where the evaluated activity takes place, whereas traditional LCA is site generic. During the last few years, the release of geographical information system (GIS) software and data sets have brought new opportunities in LCA to model land-use impacts and, more generally, any other spatially dependent impact category.

7.13 WATER USE

Water is a renewable resource, which thanks to the water cycle does not disappear. It is a resource different from any other for two main reasons: because it is essential for human and ecosystem life and because its functions are directly linked to geographic and seasonal availability since transporting it is often difficult and costly. There is sufficient water on our planet to meet the current needs of ecosystems and humans. About 119,000 km^3 of water are received every year on land in different forms of precipitation, out of which 62 percent is sent back directly to the atmosphere via evaporation and plant transpiration. Out of the remaining 38 percent, human use uses only about 3 percent, out of which 2.1 percent is used for agriculture, 0.6 percent for industrial use, and 0.3 percent for domestic uses.

However, despite these small fractions, there are still important issues associated with the water availability. Many important rivers are running dry from overuse, including industries and human beings affecting local aquatic and terrestrial ecosystems. Humans have consumed ground water so heavily in some regions and sometimes leading to exchange of water rights is an issue between two areas. It is a problem by stating there is a water scarcity in many places but the crisis is not about having too little water to satisfy our needs it is a crisis off managing water so badly that billions of people and the environment suffer badly in addition to the current mismanagement of water which is strongly linked to the competing demand for human use and ecosystem. Human demand is only increasing, namely due to growing population and changing diets with increasing meat consumption; water availability is also changing due to climate change aggravating droughts and flooding. Hence, there are further increases in the gap between the demand and availability in many of highly populated regions around the world. The problem associated with the water is dependent on where and when quality water is available. It is required to be considered when we assess the potential impact of human freshwater use on the environment including human health in life cycle assessment studies.

8 Life Cycle Interpretation

8.1 INTRODUCTION

Interpretation is the most important phase of LCA, where the result of the other phases is considered together and analyzed in the light of uncertainty of applied data and the assumptions that have been made and documented throughout the study. The outcome of the interpretation should be conclusion or recommendation. The intention of the goal definition and the restriction that this imposed on the study are to be considered. But the scope of definition and appropriateness of functional unit and system boundaries are to be considered. The interpretation should present the conclusion of LCA in an understandable way and help the user of this study appraise their robustness and potential weakness in the light of identified study limitations. Central elements of the interpretation phase such as sensitivity analysis and uncertainty analysis are also applied throughout the LCA process together with impact assessment tools as a part of iterative loops, which are used in the boundary and collection of inventory and impact assessment data. However, detailed analysis of these elements is required to proceed through the various steps. The significant issue and key process is essential until the most important elementary flow from the other phases of the LCA identified. These issues are evaluated with regard to the influence on overall results of the LCA and the completeness and consistency, and the results of the evolution are used in the formulation of conclusion and recommendation from the study. In cases where the study involves comparison of two or more systems there are additional considerations to be included in the interpretation.

8.2 IDENTIFICATION OF ISSUES

The purpose of the first element of life cycle interpretation is to analyze the result of earlier phases of the LCA to determine the most environmentally critical issues. Mostly those issues are having potential to impact on the results of the LCA. The significant issues can be methodological choices and assumptions and inventory data for important life cycle processes, and/or characterization, normalization, and weighting factors used in the impact assessment. The practitioner is encouraged to prepare a list of such choices during the practical execution of the LCA, the definition of goal and scope, the modeling of the product system and the impact assessment, to help with their identification. The sensitivity analysis can be performed as a contribution analysis where the contribution from each process or stage to total results of an impact category is qualified and expressed. It can also be done, where the processes or stages are ranked according to their relative share in the total impact. The identification of significant issues draws on the sensitivity analysis activity in the evolution element of the interpretation

DOI: 10.1201/9781003206750-8

81

82   Life Cycle Assessment

phase. In combination with information about the potential key assumption and uncertainty ranges for potential key number inventory analysis and impact assessment at the same time the evolution element takes the identified significant issues as an important input. The two elements are thus performed in the iteration in most of the cases on the life cycle impacts.

8.3 EVALUATION

The evolution element establishes the basis for the conclusion and recommendation that can be formulated in the final element of the interpretation. It is performed in an iterative interaction with the identification of key issues to determine the reliability and stability of the result from the fidelity action element. Like the identification of key issues, the evolution covers the result from the earlier phases of LCA and the inventory analysis and the impact assessment in accordance with the goal and scope of the study with focus on significant issues identified among the methodological choices and data. The outcome of evaluation is crucial to determine the state of the conclusion and recommendation from the study and it must therefore be presented in a way that gives the project team leader and user of the study a clear understanding of the outcome. The evaluation involves a completeness check, sensitivity analysis in combination with the uncertainty analysis, and a consistency check.

8.4 SENSITIVITY CHECK

The sensitivity check has the purpose of identifying the key processes and most important elementary flows as those elements that contribute most to the overall impacts from the product system. Sensitivity analysis can be performed and presented as a contribution analysis to see which activities contribute to which environmental impact scores by how much and through which elementary flow analysis to see which activities contribute most to which impact or flows for a detail sensitivity analysis and how it is performed. In support of the iterative approach applied in LCA, sensitivity analysis is also used as a steering activity in the iteration loops that are performed throughout the LCA in support of boundary setting for a product system, inventory data collection, and impact assessment. The findings from these earlier sensitivity analyses are brought into the sensitivity check of the interpretation phase. In the interpretation phase, sensitivity analysis is used together with the information about the uncertainty of significant issues among inventory data, impact assessment data, and methodological assumptions and choices to assess the reliability of the results, conclusion, and recommendation.

The influence of data uncertainty of key issues can be checked by allowing the data to vary within the limits given by the uncertainty estimates while modeling the product system and checking the results. If the information about the stochastic uncertainties, of the individual elementary flow and characterization factor allows it, is also possible to calculate the uncertainty of the result in terms of inventory and environmental impacts. Methodical systematic uncertainty can be checked by analyzing different choices, applied allocation principle as a scenario, and reporting the

Life Cycle Interpretation

influence on the results. Methodological choices that may be relevant to include in a sensitivity analysis include handling and multifunctional processes, system expansion assumption or allocation rules, cutoff criteria boundary setting and system definition, and judgments and assumption concerning data in the inventory and for the impact assessment selection of impact category, calculation of category indicator results characterization and normalization and weighting of the impacts scores. The combination of sensitivity analysis and the uncertainty analysis helps identify focus points for improved inventory data collection or impact assessment.

8.5 CONSISTENCY CHECK

The consistency check is performed to investigate whether the assumptions, method, and data that have been applied in the study are consistent with the goal and scope. If there is difference in the quality of inventory data along a product life cycle and between different product systems consistent with the significance of the processes. The data represent based on the goal and scope of the study. Inventory data quality concerns both the time-related, geographical, and technological representativeness of the data, the appropriateness of the chosen unit process to represent the process of the product system, and the uncertainty of the data. In case of comparisons between different product systems the consistency check also investigates whether allocation rules and system boundary setting as well as impact assessment have been consistently applied to all compared product systems. When inconsistencies are identified, their influence on the results of the study is evaluated and considered in order to draw conclusions from the result.

8.6 INTERPRETATION

In studies that involve a comparison of a product system the interpretation must consider several additional points to ensure fair and relevant conclusions from the study. Significant issues must be determined for each of the systems, and special attention should be given to the issues that differ between the system and that have the potential to change the balance of the comparison. The completeness check must have specific focus on differences in the completeness of the treatment of some of the significant issues between the product systems. If there are differences that could influence the comparison results, these should be eliminated if possible and otherwise be kept in mind in the formulation of conclusions. If an uncertainty analysis is performed to investigate whether the difference between two systems is statistically significant, the analysis should be performed on the difference between the system, one system minus the other, which should be checked for statistically significant differences from zero considering potential covariation between processes of two systems, processes which are the same. When an LCA is intended to be used in a comparative assertion that is to be disclosed to the public, the ISO 14044 standard requires that the evaluation element include interpretative statements based on detailed sensitivity analysis. It is emphasized in the standard that the inability of a statistical analysis to find

84   Life Cycle Assessment

significant difference between different studied alternatives does not automatically lead to the conclusion that such differences do not exist, only that the study is not able to show them significant way. A consistency check must be performed of the treatment of the key assumptions and methodological choices in the different systems to avoid a bias and ensure a fair comparison.

8.7 CRITICAL REVIEW

Around the globe, numerous LCA studies have been published and many of them based on the highest standards of quality and robustness, but there are also an alarming number of studies that contain either important mistakes or plain manipulation to obtain an intended result that would support a specific, predefined claim. These mistakes and manipulations may be stable and difficult to detect but can also be immediately identifiable to the trained eye, and a number of studies based on surprisingly blunt and evident manipulation have been published over the years. In particular, some alias studies have become classic and illustrative examples in LCA teaching of how not to do LCA comparative environmental claims in general and they also nicely illustrate the purpose and need for critical review of published LCA studies.

Critical review of any LCA study is useful in all cases where quality, robustness, and trust in results are required. Whether or not a review is required depends on the goal definition that is intended application and decision contexts, the reason for carrying out the study, and the intended audience. ISO 14044-2006 recommends the use of critical reviews in general and make them mandatory for LCA studies where results are intended to be used to support a comparative assertion intended to be disclosed to the public. These mandatory critical reviews must be performed by a panel of interested parties, including at least three invited experts. A comparative assertion is defined by ISO 14040-2006 as an environmental claim regarding the superiority or equivalence of one product versus a competing product that performs the same function. However, this definition may not be broad enough. In the European context the product environmental footprint (PEF) is an example of an LCA that will typically be subject to such review requirements. Even though a comparative assertion is not explicitly stated in the report, an environmental product declaration (EPD) and PEF aim to give data and information to be used in comparisons and they could therefore be regarded as a basis for the comparative assertions. In fact, a critical review by at least one independent and qualified external reviewer is mandatory in the PEF methodology.

The conclusion should be drawn in an iterative way. Based on the identification of significant issues and the evaluation of these for completeness, sensitivity, and consistency, preliminary conclusions can be drawn. It is then checked whether these preliminary conclusions are in accordance with the requirement of the scope definition of this study, in particular, data quality requirements, predefined assumptions and values, and limitations in methodology. If the conclusions are aligned with the requirements, they can be reported as conclusions, otherwise they must be reformulated and checked again. Recommendations based on the conclusion of the study should be logical and reasonable consequence of the conclusions.

9 Case Studies of Different Countries

9.1 USA

The high demand for cement base material to support building and infrastructure systems is of growing concern as the production of cement leads to significant GHG emissions and notable resource consumption. Efficiency of cement usage has been studied to mitigate GHG burdens, by increasing durability of cement. The implication of using cement for a longer in-use residence time was quantitatively explored. In the United States, a study was conducted on dynamic material flow analysis models to quantify the new stock of cement from 1900 to 2015. With this model the implication of increasing or decreasing mean longevity in new cement products are required. The potential implication of extending the longevity of cement is in use. Before removal of setting the cement and cement base material demand was explored in this US. LCA study several key findings from this work included a 50 percent increase in cement durability could have led to 14 percent reduction in material resource demand and also GHG emission from concrete production in USA. It is equivalent to 0.28 to 0.83 Gt of aggregates, IE+06 to 2,3E+06 TJ of energy and 0.4 to 0.7 Gt of CO_2-eq emissions. Improving durability and longevity of cement could be a critical means of mitigating environmental impacts.

9.2 UK

In UK, an integrated LCA modeling approach study was carried out for value assessment focusing on resource recovery from waste. The method tracks and forecasts a range of values across environmental, social, economic, and technical domains by attaching these two-material flow does build upon integrating unidimensional model such as material flow analysis and LCA. The usual classification of metrics into these separate domains is useful for interpreting the outputs of multidimensional assessments, but unnecessary for modeling.

UK concrete and cement industry has studied the aggregate impact that may flow and increase use of low carbon fuels. This model may investigate tipping points in this case the upstream condition under which total GHG emissions rise due to impacts downstream of electricity production. The case also highlights the contentious nature of allocation decision, and they need to examine sociopolitical imperatives the weather this framing of the case study leads to investigate how potential knew international trade links may induce further offshoring of environmental and social impacts.

Finally, the study indicates that these systematic multidimensional changes may be understood as being driven by changes in the technical value of resource flows

DOI: 10.1201/9781003206750-9

more broadly the result highlights the advantage of approaching such analysis with an intention to make high-level interferences of complex system including important interaction between background and distributional effects and so forth, rather than taking market centric approach and devoting disproportionate attention to optimizing in come durable sets of outputs using limited one strains in this study.

It is only beginning to prove that these issues require a comprehensive treatment of such effect this approach aims to address a number of shortcomings simpler than the approach of sustainability assessment in general. It is equally demandingly in terms of data input requirements also of important is omission of any treatment of uncertainty of which robust analysis complemented by sensitivity analysis is necessary for any comprehensive sustainability analysis. The modeling challenges include questions regarding how to value fix capital long lasting plan infrastructure our account of discrete parents disruptive technical transitions there are also issues relating to a wider framework within which the model is intended to explain how to select appropriate metrics for the evaluation assessment and usually how to integrate the results across the various domains in such a way that outcome can be optimized by a set of criteria that remains totally transparent clearly there are many difficult conceptual and technical challenges to overcome and these are an ongoing focus. but the challenge of adapting such transparent and provocative approach into a political decision having these displays such a cost benefit analysis that picked out is single objective number even greater. As the construction industry begins to shift towards more sustainable business models and government legislation becomes more stringent for industry in terms of sustainable practices, it is imperative that those educated with working experience and environment proficient can enter industry with this skill knowledge and awareness of not only their chosen profession but also how they can apply sustainability into everyday working to align with the ever-changing business strategy.

9.3 SPAIN

A life cycle assessment of the Spanish cement industry is seeking to find out hot spots depending on the impact categories after analysis, as it was due to fossil fuel combustion, use of electricity, and mining in quarry. CO_2 generated from processed limestone's calcination has impact on climate change. It is also remarkable that alternative fuel combustion is still low and material pretreatment and transportation are minimal. Going beyond the hot spot recognition, this study has explored the Spanish cement sector in 2010 studied for the future. Consequently a variety of scenarios were developed in order to implement BAT and other technical solutions that would promote reduction in emissions waste and energy consumption. Most significant improvements are referred to the energy requirement both the clinkerization in kiln and power consumption to face these challenges. It is needed to improve the redesign the kiln feed and, on the other hand, both raw material and fossil fuel substitution scenario are the best option to achieve less impact. The second hot spot identified for changing the primary material enter in

Case Studies of Different Countries 87

the cement mill with clinker by secondary blending materials previously considered waste like fly ash, blast furnace slag, and silica sand. It leads to 10 to 13 percent reduction in each impact category furthermore using alternate fuel instead of fossil as shown in its advantage decreasing 37 and 33 percentage in acidification and photo chemical ozone formation, respectively, but increasing 10 percent Fresh water eutrophication. Finally in an ideal scenario where all technological options are implemented, reduction would reach from 21 percent in climate change to 49 percent in acidification. On this sectorial approach to the Spanish cement industry, it is possible to conclude that to face the problem derived from the fossil fuel combustion a fuel shift is needed. Material substitution is another satisfactory solution for the industry in terms of impact, but it requires a change in the demand and further investigation.

9.4 BRAZIL

An LCA study was carried out in Brazil, as a large environmental impact is generated by their cement industry throughout the life cycle of the product. Its results showed that during life cycle of Portland cement, the industrial process impacts the environment where the greener gas affect which is caused by the combustion of fossil fuel and due to calcination was highlighted. There is air containment by heavy metals due to mining activity and small caused by emission of particulate matter the current production in present model is an example of situation that in near future could culminate with end of natural resource and a complete change world environment. This situation can be avoided by replacing fossil fuel by use of agricultural wastes and its residues can decrease use of cement in concrete for the reduction of CO_2 emissions. The World Economic model of mass production and goods consumption is growing by inclusion of the BRICs (Brazil, Russia, India, and China) but also Thailand, South Africa, Turkey, and other consumers in the global market. The search for technological development and economic growing are providing the generation of less durable goods and a market that strives to meet this demand without restriction. This causes mainly the extinction of natural resources and environmental degradation such situation that requires modification in relationship between the industrial society and the nature before the occurrence of irreversible damages sustainable development constitutes a proposal that seeks to change the production system supplying the needs of society and ensuring preservation of natural resources.

LCA is one of the main methods used to evaluate impacts caused by industrial products. Cement process production can generate local environmental impacts such as noise, reduced air quality, and changes in local ecosystems due to extraction of raw material such as clay, limestone, and others. Regionally it can cause acid rain due to emission of sulfur dioxide and nitrogen oxide, among others. Already the burning of fossil fuels like oil, coal, and natural gas, have caused climate change worldwide. According to the International Energy Agency, cement production generates a global average CO_2 emission of 0.81 kg.kg^{-1} of cement produced. On average about 1 tonne of concrete is produced each year for all human beings around the world. It is estimated that 5 percent of global CO_2 emissions come from the manufacture of cement. Besides the generation of CO_2 in the process of manufacturing of cement are produced million tons of waste particular matter from the cement kiln each year that contribute to pollution and respiratory health risk. The calcination process of obtaining CaO from $CaCO_3$ generates CO_2 and contributes to about half the CO_2 emitted, while the rest comes from the energy consumption during the production process.

The characteristics of technological process and physiochemical and toxicological properties of raw materials inputs used in cement manufacturing are vital for clinker and cement. The cement plant causes a risk to the health of workers, public health, and the environment. It is associated with the exposure of particulate matter that permeates the entire chain of production and emission of pollutants that occur continuously that even small concentrations contribute to the chronic risk. It can be seeing that all stages of cement manufacturing generate impact to the environment. It is also noted that so much of the energy used in the process focuses on the step of reduction measures.

9.5 SWITZERLAND

The Swiss cement industry produces 4 million tonnes of cement per year. The manufacturing of cement is very energy intensive. The energy requirement lies between 4200 and 5000 MJ/t, whereas about 3500 MJ/t is the thermal energy used in the elevated temperature clinker burning process. Energy carriers have traditionally been fossil fuels such as a coal and heavy fuel oil. Increasingly distinct kinds of waste oil, dried sewage sledge, plastic waste, or waste solvent are used as alternate fuels in the cement industry. In 2010–2012 the share of alternate fuel amounted to 52.8 percent of total thermal energy consumption. This fraction is supposed to increase even more in the future. Swiss cement industry has studied the development of various alternate fuel consumption in the cement kiln. Slowly it has increased over the years where solvent is welcome as an alternate fuel for the cement industry in Switzerland. It is comparably pure, easy to manage, and it usually has a high energy content. A share of 13.6 percent of the total alternate fuel is used till 2018.

The results from the case studies showed that solvent incineration in clinker kilns has a net environmental benefit, at least if the heating value and therefore the amount of substituted fossil fuel is sufficiently high, and the pollutant content is small. One such model of solvent incineration in special solvent incineration plant has already been set up.

9.6 INDONESIA

The environmental impact study was carried out using life cycle assessment cement industry in Indonesia. In 2010, the rapid development in Indonesia caused some demand on the cement industry to produce more cement for domestic needs. Cement is made by means of mining of limestone and fuel for production process

Case Studies of Different Countries

that involves pyro processing and grinding process in its activity to be able to produce cement. These activities produce emission of CO_2, NOx, SOx and particulate matter. These emission have an impact on global warming and decreasing ambient air quality, which has an impact on human health and the environment. This Indonesian study identifies the impact of main process based on the cradle to great approach starting from the process of exploitation of raw materials to the production process that produces cement as the main product the impact identification was done by using LCA method with the help of the software SimaPro 8.5.2. The LCIA category includes global warming potential for 100 years, acidification, and carcinogens. The method used was TRACI, a midpoint approach. Results after normalization show that the highest impacts generated were global warming from the kiln process, acidification from the kiln process, and carcinogens from the raw mill process.

The impact that arose from each process had a different magnitude depending on the material input, fuel, energy used, emission released and the production process that occurred. Several types of impact that arose needed to be analyzed more deeply to interpret the data on the SimaPro application with existing data of exploitation and production of cement. The purpose of this interpretation was to find out hot spots with the greatest impact from a series of processes of cement exploitation and production. Impact hot spots are the biggest impact points in a process. Because the process between one unit and another is different, there will be differences in the value of the impact produced in each cement production process.

The impact value is influenced by input data at the LCI stage. Input data are in the form of type of raw material used, type of fuel, type of energy, and emission produced along with the quantity. The value in the normalization stage is used as a reference to find out the greatest impact because at the characterization stage each impact has a different unit, so that the impact cannot be compared between one another. In the normalization stage, equalization of all types of impacts is carried out. The value obtained from the normalization stage is the result of the value in the characterization stage divided by the normalization factor. The hot spot point of impact of global warming was found to be the kiln. It is influenced using fuel in the form of coal as well as several alternate fuels. The kiln unit produces the largest GHG emissions of all the units. The cement production was analyzed using LCA methods on a normal category impact, global warming, acidification, and carcinogens. The environmental impact is correlated with its input and output from each process in the cement production.

9.7 CZECH REPUBLIC

An LCA study was taken up in the Czech Republic, where substantial progress has been made in degrees of environmental impacts of cement production. Dust pollution around the cement plant has been decreased due to efficient dust separators. Further emission reduction has been studied via LCA. The environmental burden of cement production was also decreased by substitution of cement by alternate binders. Hydraulic properties of energy by-products have been investigated for a long time to check their potential as a partial substitute for traditional cement binders. The study has focused on examining the influence of variation of concrete composition on the environmental impact's identification of the most severe procedures in this cement production analysis of meaningfulness of implementation of the proposed measures. The environment is a complex system. Potential modification of concrete composition or production technology may bring benefits to certain areas and on the contrary may cause environmental harm from another perspective. Hence, analysis of similar production impacts cannot be based on one aspect, and a broad profile of impact categories will be assessed regarding the concrete production and its total burden.

The results presented in the study were that a partial replacement of cement with fly ash decreases the consumption of raw materials and significantly reduces the emission of harmful substances. Although not that extensively, the application of selective noncatalytic reduction (SNCR) reduces most of the environmental impact as well. Compared to fly ash substitution, the NO_x reduction affects the eutrophication of the environment. As previously mentioned, the NO_x reduction technology used during the combustion process negatively affects the fly ash in terms of grain morphology and chemical composition. Based on the assessment presented in the study, replacement of cement with fly ash seems to positively interfere with more of the environmental impact categories than the investigated NO_x reduction process. So, the partial replacement of cement, the highly energetically demanding material, with untreated fly ash could be a more efficient approach to sustainable development. However, the SNCR method may be more advantageous in locations where the eutrophication of water and soil is the main environmental problem.

9.8 CHINA

China produces cement to the tune of 2.4 billion tonnes per annum, which is more than 50 percent of world cement production. In the past decade, China has been more conscious of cement production and its environmental impacts. Chinese cement production has challenges and opportunities using LCA to understand the embodied energy environmental impact and potential energy saving of manufacture products has become more widespread among researchers in recent years. A recent LCA study of China's and other countries' cement industry provides an assessment of methodology used by the researcher compared to ISO LCA standards like ISO 14040-2006 and ISO 14044-2006. In order to evaluate whether the study provides information on the intended application, target audience, functional unit, system boundary, data sources, data quality assessment, data compilation, and other elements and draw conclusion regarding the level of attendance to ISO standard for this study review, it is found that Chinese researchers have gained much experience during last decade but still have room for improvement in establishing boundaries, assessing data quality, identifying data sources, etc.

Case Studies of Different Countries

Life cycle assessment is a valuable tool for understanding total energy consumption, identifying energy saving opportunities and information for decision makers regarding policies and energy efficient investments. Recently there have been several LCA studies conducted by Chinese scholars focusing on China's cement industry. LCA to evaluate this industry has played a significant role in generating increased understanding of all its impacts as well as energy saving and emission reduction opportunities.

The quality of LCA study in Chinese industry, corporations, and associations has improved by participating in assessment and collaboration with LCA researcher of other countries. Government could support healthier research by subsidizing pilot projects LCA is also be linked with energy audits and broader energy management.

9.9 GERMANY

An LCA of building materials in Germany was conducted by the German Building Materials Association. The LCA is an appropriate tool for supporting environmentally oriented studies. With this method, a variety of impacts can be covered taking into consideration the entire life cycle of a product. Appropriate application of method provides quality results which are universally accepted following the internationally standardized procedure. Despite the standard procedure in conducting LCA differences in respect to the industrial sector do exit hence the goal of the building material association is to summarize standardize requirement of healthier building components. A first guideline for conducting inventory analysis is in the plan of the building material industry. Based on the guideline, the requirement of an impact assessment and interpretation with LCA in the building material industry is the essential step. The procedure emphasizes that the possibility of limitation LCA is also seen. The life cycle assessment is a suitable tool for analyzing and assessing the impacts that are caused through production, use, and disposal of products or product system. For specific applications LCA does not produce clear-cut, straightforward assertions but gives diverse and complex results. It supports the process of decision-making by rendering complex issues transparent. The concepts of LCA are mainly concerned with basic aspects like the observation of the whole life cycle of a product from raw material acquisition processing and production to reuse, recycling, and disposal and the recoveries of all these impacts associated with the life cycle of the environment such as raw material and energy and use of land for construction of building area. Assessment of these impacts in view of possible effects on the environment-oriented decisions the main emphasis in the field of impact analysis and interpretation. The LCA is meant to assist conducting the methodology and the critical study of existing analysis the focus is on the building and construction industry. It follows the guidelines of conducting inventory analysis in plants and building industry many different questions can arise in the building construction industry which can be tackled by using LCA method different functional limits are possible depending on the goal of the study.

9.10 INDIA

LCA is used to enhance environmental management, particularly when used in conjunction with EMSs. There are several areas where LCA can be helpful: in the identification of significant environmental effects, in the quantification of those effects, in the assessment of changes in environmental performance, and the environmental benefits arising from changes in operating conditions, equipment, procedures, raw materials, or alternate products specifically for blended cement. The cement industry is faced with many challenges that span the product/process life cycle. On the one hand the cement industry itself is challenged by several significant environmental issues like carbon dioxide and NO_x emissions and production energy requirements. On the other hand, studies indicate that certain aspects of air pollution are due to fugitive dust, land degradation, and captive limestone mines as well as power plants.

Limestone mining, cement manufacturing, and their CPPs are bound together in the LCA of energy use and emissions. Many companies around the globe are reexamining their business operations and relationships in a fundamental way. They are exploring the concept of sustainable development, seeking to integrate their pursuit of profitable growth with the assurance of environmental protection and quality of life for present and future generations. Based on this new perspective, some companies are beginning to make significant changes in their policies, commitments, and business strategies.

LCA attempts to provide a systematic approach to quantifying resource consumption and environmental releases to air, water, and soil associated with products, processes, and services. It takes into consideration that all product life cycle stages, extracting and processing raw materials, manufacturing, transportation and distribution, use/reuse, and recycling and waste management, have environmental and economic impacts. The Indian cement industry ranks second in the world in cement production. It is currently in search of competitive advantages for continuous improvement in terms of environmental concerns—the ecological degradation of mined out areas of raw materials, air pollution due to both fugitive and stack dust, and GHG emissions.

Hence, to improve the environment, one needs to reduce both thermal and electrical consumption, which has a direct bearing on the environment. There is an urgent need to adopt a holistic integrated approach like LCA to identify weaker subunits or the processes to deal both in terms of energy consumption (i.e., cost) as well as on an environmental front as with dust and GHG emissions. It is true that growing awareness of the environmental problems and cost-effective compulsion has led cement plants to adopt advanced technology in mining, crushing, grinding, and pyro-processing technology along with environmental operational control and process optimization measures. The LCA of the construction industry specifically for commercial buildings has been studied in India. The life cycle of a building starts from the exaction and mining of raw materials and minerals, encompasses various production stages of building material, transportation of those materials to the building construction site, and construction of the building

Case Studies of Different Countries

structure using those materials, water, and energy. The construction phase is followed by use and operation up to final disposal of demolition of waste from the building either to recycling or to the landfill. As the life span of the primary material used in the construction of the building (i.e., mainly concrete) is expected to be 80 years, but depending on the use and operation phases of the building may last up to 50 years. After the end of the use and operation phase of the building, the structure may be demolished, and the debris is disposed of to recycling and some of the residuals go to landfills and dumps. Thus, the life cycle of the building ends with the final disposal of the demolished debris of the building. Hence, the life cycle of a building can be divided into four major phases: construction phase, operation (use) phase, maintenance phase, and demolition phase.

9.10.1 BUILDING CONSTRUCTION

The decisions made at the time of construction of the building will influence the environmental impact potentials associated with the life cycle of a building. The materials consumed during the construction phase will not only have an impact during the construction phase but also have far reaching effects on the other phases of the building. Construction activity includes site preparation, construction of foundation, superstructure, mechanical, electrical equipment installations, and interior finishing. The construction phase of a commercial building involves large quantities of building materials. This phase includes production of building materials, burdens from energy used for power tools and lighting as well as diesel fuel used by equipment at the construction site and associated transportation of the construction material from factory to the construction site. Data related to the construction process of the commercial building and transportation distances of construction materials to the construction site were obtained from the construction company using an LCA questionnaire and discussions held with the contractors.

9.10.2 BUILDING OPERATION

After completion of the construction phase and occupation of the office and building spaces by the occupants, the operation use phase of the building starts. This phase extends up to the end of the life of the building. In the study in India, the life cycle of the building was considered as 50 years. However, it may be possible that the building may continue to serve its occupants even after its assumed to be at the end of its life. The commercial building normally operates for six days in a week for 12 hours daily. There may be some commercial building that work for 24 hours depending on the usage and type of commercial activities carried out in those buildings. This phase of a building's life cycle may account for 60 to 80 percent of the impact associated with the life cycle of a building. The operation phase includes interior and exterior lighting of the building, water supply to the occupants, and waste and wastewater management, energy requirements for cooling, ventilation of the building, and equipment operation. For housekeeping operation, material used for housekeeping such as phenol and soaps are used, and their inventories are accounted for in the impact assessment. In the Indian study, it was assumed that only electricity from thermal plants was used as grid power; for other type of power generated for electricity from diesel set inside the compound of the building has not been considered, as seldom DG set power was used. The energy consumption of the building during the operation phase was based on the data provided by the construction company and on the daily usage pattern of the building (daily usage was considered to be about 12 hours a day, six days a week). Actual electricity consumption records for the buildings were also considered. One of the major assumptions of the study is that material used for building service such as wires, power cables, AC ductwork, chillers, and electricity boards were not considered under the scope of the study.

9.10.3 BUILDING MAINTENANCE

Construction materials have a service life and need replacement after the end of their use/service life. The service life of a building as discussed earlier is assumed to be 50–80 years and, of course, depends upon the structural components and its maintenance. However, about other materials used in the construction of the building structure, they may require a quote for replacement. Frequent maintenance requirements in a building are painting, which is required after every four to five years, plywood, and so forth. For commercial buildings such as office buildings and retail malls, interior design and decoration usually changes with the choice of the occupant. However, in the Indian study it was assumed that the occupant remained the same for the entire life cycle of the building. Emissions from the maintenance stage were computed based on the life span of materials, and it was assumed that 10 percent of the building material used during the construction phase was used again during the maintenance phase. For paint, it was assumed that the painting of the building was carried out twice in ten years and that plywood would be replaced twice within 50 years.

9.10.4 BUILDING DEMOLITION

The last phase of a building's life involves demolition and disassembling of the structure. The conventional demolition and decommissioning process often results in the disposal of the majority of the materials and debris to the landfill and dumps. The demolition waste of economic material is recycled, such as reinforced steel bars and aluminum items. The debris, comprising demolished concrete, broken bricks, broken glass, and other waste material, are presently partially recycled and disposed of in nearby areas. The impacts related to the demolition phase of a building are due to energy consumption and emission associated with the demolition machinery as well as the energy required for the transportation of the demolition materials from the building site to the recycling facility. Due to lack of an appropriate mechanism, some of the materials are not 100 percent recycled in India. For alternate paths for future building, it is suggested

Case Studies of Different Countries

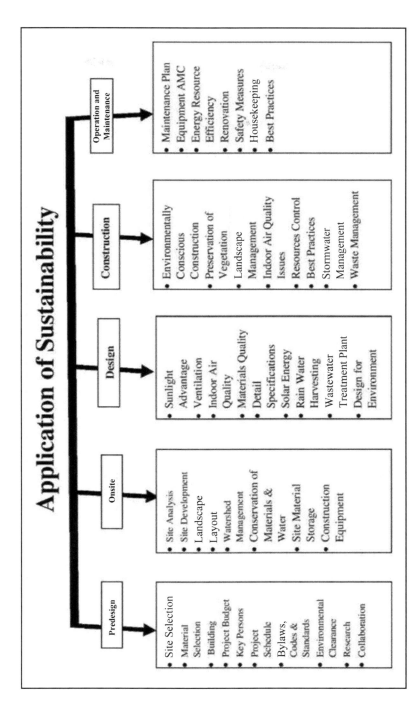

FIGURE 9.1 Application of sustainability for the construction industry.

that a majority of the waste generated from the demolition of a building would be utilized as a recycled sand and aggregate. The emissions avoided by use of construction and demolished waste recycled materials due to saving of virgin materials will result in negative impacts for all impact potentials. Sustainability for the construction industry is pivotal role to play for improving environment at the same time reducing impact, adopting systematic LCA application for construction industry.

Figure 9.1 highlights few points and explains the sustainability of the construction industry and the relevance of its applications. Under the predesign stage there are a number of aspects to cover like material selection, building program, project budget, team selection, partnering, project schedule, bylaws, codes, and standards. Onsite decisions cover site analysis, site development, the layout of water bodies and management and consumption of material and water resources, and site material handling with different equipment. Under the design, the heading needs to design for solar energy input, the addition of newer materials and their specification improving the indoor air quality and better landscape. Under the head of construction during construction efforts should be made serious efforts to reduce environmental issues, be conscious of materials and their quality, improve air quality and maximum use of daylight, minimize the waste at the site, indoor air quality, green belt development, indoor air quality management, and resource control and best practices adopted during construction. Under the operation and maintenance heading, there are key factors like housekeeping, best practices, repair, and renovation resources efficiency, energy-saving, improvement in indoor air quality maintaining maintenance schedules.

10 Future Challenges for Life Cycle Assessment

10.1 AWARENESS OF LIFE CYCLE THINKING

Life cycle thinking awareness among general students is becoming necessary around the world. In fact, irrespective of faculty the basics of LCT and its relevant related fields/tools should be taught in the colleges and universities. Educating people for more sustainable ways to relate to our habitat involves preparing us to adopt LCA, LCC, SLCA, and OLCA for sustainable practices for products or services that reduce the impact on climate change and the impact of climate change in our lives. LCT aims to increase the sustainability of a product or system along its entire value chain by reducing environmental impacts and at the same time increasing socioeconomic performance (UNEP 2020). LCA primarily focuses on environmental impacts alone (ISO 14040/14044-2006), assessing quantitatively the environmental impacts of products and services along their value chains. Over the past decades, methodological developments in the direction of environmental and societal LCC, SLCA, and LCSA have also been made, as have numerous differentiation and brandings, including carbon and water footprints (ISO 14067-2018; ISO 14046-2014) and the EU's PEF and Organization Environmental Footprint (EC JRC 2020; Bach et al. 2018; Pant et al. 2012). In the following, the term LCA is used in a broad sense and captures these different concepts and methodologies.

These practices may be individual, in the choices we make about our own consumption and lifestyle for example slowing down population growth, consuming a diet with a smaller carbon footprint or using renewable energies, or consuming less; or they may be collective, the result of choices one makes as citizens when participating in the democratic process at various levels of government, or when one influences the behavior of corporations, for example, by adopting caps on emissions or a carbon tax, or incentivizing the reliance on clean energies. Government policies such as caps on emissions are essential to slowing global warming, and they are subject to influence and preferences by citizens, educated to understand the scientific consensus on climate change and with the capacity to exercise influence as citizens. Collective responses may also include shaping the way in which we live and our habitats, for instance the value we assign to nature as we design and build the homes and cities where we live and work.

In addition to personal responsibility for our individual impact on climate change, and participation in collective processes that support systemic changes in the norms and institutions that undergird climate change, slowing down and perhaps over time reverting climate change requires also advancing knowledge and

DOI: 10.1201/9781003206750-10

98 Life Cycle Assessment

inventing technologies that can help us transform our interactions with the environment, in a way helping us reinvent our way of life, and so educating for LCA and its related tools for sustainable development becomes necessary. Sustainability involves equipping people with the ethical frameworks, the imagination, and the necessary skills for such advancement of knowledge and invention. Examples of such design and invention and changes to our way of life include developing a CE with production of goods next to cities to reduce transportation costs, synergizing among industries to use one industry's waste or by-products in other industries, as well as urbanization with populations concentrated in sustainable cities.

10.2 MITIGATION OF CLIMATE CHANGE

Climate change mitigation policies have been implemented in five major emitting economies—China, the European Union, India, Japan, and the United States— while analyzing their historical performance in terms of energy system and greenhouse gas emissions indicators. In cases where policies aim to reduce future emissions, their target performance levels are assessed. The review centers on the sectors of electricity generation, passenger vehicles, freight transport, forestry, industry, buildings, agriculture, and oil and gas production. Most focus countries have implemented successful policies for renewable energy, fuel efficiency, electrification of passenger vehicles, and forestry. For other sectors, information is limited or very heterogeneous (e.g., buildings, appliances, agriculture) or there are few comprehensive policies in place (e.g., industry). The article further presents an explorative emissions scenario developed under the assumption that all countries will replicate both the observed trends in sector-level indicators and the trends that policies for future emissions reductions aspire to achieve. It shows that the global replication of sector progress would reduce GHG emissions by 2030 by about 20 percent compared to a current policies scenario.

All countries analyzed would overachieve the emissions reduction targets in their post-2020 climate targets. However, the resulting reduction in global emissions by 2030 would still not be sufficient to keep the world on track for a global cost-effective pathway that keeps the temperature from increasing less than 2°C. The findings of this study emphasize the need for transformative policies to keep the Paris Agreement temperature limit within reach.

10.3 GLOBALIZATION

LCA will be elaborated in many directions in the next decade. Regionalized databases will be developed, new impact assessment methods will be designed, and methods for uncertainty analysis will be improved. However, more fundamentally, it is believed that the next decade of the 21st century will be the decade of life cycle sustainability analysis. In this decade LCSA will hopefully develop offering a framework for questions at diverse levels of products, sectors, and economies and for addressing these questions to the full sustainability scope engulfing people, planet, and prosperity and to a more complete set of mechanisms. Unlike

Future Challenges for LCA

LCA, LCSA is a framework of models rather than a model in itself: a transdisciplinary integration framework for disciplinary models and methods, selected and interlinked for addressing and answering a specific life cycle sustainability question. LCSA is a framework for looking from one viewpoint (i.e., the life cycle viewpoint) to sustainability questions and only providing life cycle answers and no others; risk assessment is, for example, not part of this framework.

However, risk assessment is truly relevant for certain sustainability questions and should in those cases be added to or performed instead of LCSA tools. LCSA shows similarities with the field of integrated assessment. Integrated assessment is an interdisciplinary process of combining, interpreting, and communicating knowledge from diverse scientific disciplines in such a way that the whole cause-effect chain of a problem can be evaluated. Establishing a framework for LCSA does not make present day product-oriented LCA and LCC superfluous. On the contrary, it only relates product oriented LCA and LCC to specific questions, for which these specific methods are perfectly suitable. There is still a vast amount of research needed to achieve this, for example, in relation to the choice of attributional, consequential, and scenario-based modeling of systems and related timeframes, including aspects of unpredictability of emerging systems, complex adaptive systems, and other contingencies. Elaborating the LCSA framework is a major challenge for the global scientific community together with international governmental bodies: strong international collaboration is necessary if we do not want to end up once more with a plethora of different approaches and methods.

10.4 INTEGRATION

The object of LCC analysis is to choose the most cost-effective approach from a series of alternatives so the least long-term cost of ownership is achieved. LCC analysis helps engineers justify equipment and process selection based on total costs rather than the initial purchase price of equipment or projects. Here, synergies between the environmental and economic considerations must be utilized to move towards sustainable development. There are several definitions of LCC in the design phase. However, in many instances business practices have sufficiently short perspectives that limit the time, resources, or experience to consider costs outside of the company's gate, for example regarding usage and disposal of a product. Based on the definition of goal and scope, a cost model must be developed according to the system boundaries and cost issues selected. Appropriate data must be collected or estimated (where necessary) considering the quality required. The quality and completeness of the relevant data is of highest importance for the results and should be supported by sensitivity analyses. If quantitative data on the processes and the corresponding material and energy flows from an LCA are available, then it is very efficient to base the LCC model on the life cycle inventory analysis since an existing product system model can be used. The approach taken was to assess the life cycle costs based on a life cycle inventory. The materials within the inventory were multiplied with estimated specific prices, including working and machine hours in the inventory.

100 Life Cycle Assessment

The globalization of the economy, pressing ecological issues such as climate change, and recent market demands are shaping and changing how we view the role of corporations in society. Traditionally, the role of the corporation has been understood primarily in economic terms. Companies provide products and services and, in doing so, they create jobs and wealth. Increasingly, stakeholders (shareholders, investors, communities, regulators, employees, customers, and nongovernmental organizations) are taking a broader perspective of corporate responsibility that incorporates not only economic performance, but also social, and environmental performance factors. There are four performance areas stakeholders are evaluating to determine whether a company is moving towards more sustainable business practices and whether a company is conducting its business in an ethical and socially responsible manner: environmental performance, economic performance, social performance and responsibility, and conduct and governance.

10.5 EXERGY ASSIMILATION

In most of the chemical and metallurgical processes at the manufacturing unit, the chemical exergy plays a vital role for purposes of resource accounting and environmental analysis. It is suggested that exergy is one of the most suitable indicators for both resource and emission accounting. There has been an increase in the use of natural resources for millennia, be they fossil fuels or any minerals. At the same time, enormous quantities of waste materials and effluents are released to the atmosphere, water bodies, or to land surface, effecting the delicately balanced natural cycles that make life possible on Earth. Hence use of exergy as general environmental indicator for resource accounting would improve the situation in two ways. First, an exergy balance automatically combines both mass and energy flows thus providing a concise representation of the process. This accounting becomes useful to characterize the process/product. Second, the use of exergy enables the environmentalist to take care of energy conservation and entropy covering both laws of thermodynamics in identifying areas for potential improvement. Chemical exergy content can be used as a tool for first-order evaluation of the environmental impact associated with waste effluents of any industrial process. Scope for integration of both LCA and exergy analysis will give inner picture of process or product in terms of evaluating not only environmental impact but also identifying of inefficient units or products in terms of exergy.

Though LCA is a tool of standardization and is getting established as a method for products and functions explicitly, it gives the most detailed results but becomes inconclusive on certain environmental parameters. So both LCA and exergy can work in a complementary fashion. Complementing use is not completely easy and simple but efforts should be made to facilitate the integration of both tools. One of the major benefits of integration of these tools would be to decrease the effort put into inventorying, simultaneously improving the quality of the data, and obtaining faster development of treatment data. Integration of LCA and exergy analysis includes estimation and calculations of both inputs and outputs of both raw

Future Challenges for LCA

materials and energy by summing in one unit during LCA inventory and impact analysis stage. It will identify inefficient use of natural resources and other energies like thermal and electrical. Exergy is more quantitative and precise in nature. Most critical point of exergy is that is illuminates the energy quality. However, exergy measurements are useful for only well-known systems for which detailed calculations can be modeled.

10.6 CIRCULAR ECONOMY

The current global interest in CE opens an opportunity to make society's consumption and production patterns more resource efficient. Assessing CE strategies requires addressing the technical and scientific challenges involved across the life cycle of such strategies, as well as the broader implications for the sustainability of both emerging and developed economies. LCA is a crucial assessment methodology to inform and improve CE strategies by comparing them in terms of sustainable performance. Even if the methodology is standardized (ISO 14040–14044-2006), further requirements must be set to ensure comparability between LCA studies. The same strict principles must apply to compare CE strategies based on LCA. It is very well suited to assess the sustainability impacts of CE strategies. Now we already use more resources than the planet is capable of regenerating, so we must find ways to utilize less energy, water, materials, and resources in general. In the cement industry we are searching for ways to close product life cycles, whether at the outset by using renewable energy, or at the end by using recyclable materials. We need radical innovation to develop new technologies and business models. The CE is part of the solution. Several methods of sustainable manufacturing in the cement industry have been evaluated recently in open literature and progress has been made on the research front.

Techniques such as CCS, material substitution, the use of alternative fuels and utilizing energy efficient technologies have been proposed as means of mitigating the negative environmental impact of cement production. Some firms have not fully bought into research innovations to plant scale as they are still regarded as pilot scale technologies to their conventional methods. Absorption of carbon dioxide from cement kilns by algae to generate biofuel can partially replace fuel and also reduce release of CO_2 into atmosphere. There are a number of such technology ideas available for the reduction of GHG from cement plants. Eco-friendly low-emission cements sometimes struggle to meet performance requirements and satisfy funding evaluators; thus, it is still currently an arduous task to fully commercialize these ideas. An effective CE can be planned in two ways: by raising awareness of CE opportunities in the private sector's engagement and by identifying innovative ideas to work with in collaborative efforts between cement industries and educational and R&D institutes in India. Government should be proactive in allocating funds for such innovative research projects like carbon capture and sequestration. Major players of the Indian cement industry have already committed themselves to long-term roadmaps to reducing GHG emissions, increasing resource conservation, and maximizing renewable energy use.

10.7 CARBON CAPTURE AND UTILIZATION

Carbon Capture and Utilization (CCU) is an emerging field proposed for emissions mitigation and even negative emissions. These potential benefits need to be assessed by the holistic method of LCA that accounts for multiple environmental impact categories over the entire life cycle of products or services. However, even though LCA is a standardized method, current LCA practice differs widely in methodological choices.

The resulting LCA studies show large variability which limits their value for decision support. Applying LCA to CCU technologies leads to further specific methodological issues (e.g., due to the double role of CO_2 as emission and feedstock). In this work, we therefore present a comprehensive guideline for LCA of CCU technologies. The guideline has been development in a collaborative process involving over 40 experts and builds upon existing LCA standards and guidelines. The presented guidelines should improve comparability of LCA studies through clear methodological guidance and predefined assumptions on feedstock and utilities. Transparency is increased through interpretation and reporting guidance. Improved comparability should help to strengthen knowledge-based decision-making. Consequently, research funds and time can be allocated more efficiently for the development of technologies for climate change mitigation and negative emissions.

10.8 CARBON NEUTRALITY

Carbon neutral, yes—that sounds familiar. But climate? The answer is simple: it is not just carbon dioxide, CO_2, which is driving climate change, even if it makes up 80 percent of the climate gases (including contributions from changes in land use) emitted by human activities. Carbon dioxide is the most abundant greenhouse gas we are adding to the atmosphere, but it is not the only one. The international climate change treaty, the Kyoto Protocol, limits the emissions of six main GHGs produced by human activities. The gases are carbon dioxide (CO_2), methane (CH_4), nitrous oxide (N_2O), hydrofluorocarbons (HFC), perfluorocarbons (PFC), and sulfur hexafluoride (SF_6).

Carbon neutrality is particularly challenging for the cement sector as less than 40 percent of emissions come from the energy used to produce cement. More than 60 percent of emissions come from the chemical breakdown of limestone—calcium carbonate ($CaCO_3$)—into CO_2; limestone is a calcium source that is used to produce the active component of cement—the clinker—which reacts with water at ambient temperature to produce a strong durable material. There is no practical alternative to the use of limestone due to its abundance and widespread distribution in the earth's crust. Therefore, total carbon neutrality can only be achieved by recapturing this "chemical" CO_2.

Technologies for carbon capture and storage are under development, although some technical challenges need still to be surmounted. These technologies are estimated to require large investments in terms of capital investment and in

Future Challenges for LCA

operating cost. They are also dependent on massive quantities of renewable energy to be effective. Heidelberg Cement intends to upgrade its facility in Slite on the Swedish island of Gotland to become the world's first carbon-neutral cement plant. Dalmia Cement (Bharat) have scaled up the ambitions, and now seek to be carbon negative by 2040, meaning that overall operations will be taking more CO_2 out of the atmosphere than it is produced. To meet the scale of this challenge and achieve our ambitious goal, we are exploring a number of approaches, including switching to 100 percent green fuels, including biofuels, biogas, compressed biogas (CBG) and biomass; green power generation; reducing our clinker factor in incremental stages and optimizing clinker heat consumption; switching over to solar drying for relevant raw materials; developing a new range of low-carbon cements; CCU technology; and carbon sequestration.

10.9 SUSTAINABLE CONSUMPTION AND PRODUCTION

Concerning the LCA outcomes, the determination of environmental performance is complex, and different combinations of feedstocks, conversion routes, fuels, end-use applications, and methodological assumptions may lead to a wide range of results. Different approaches are used to deal with the indirect effects which have an enormous influence on final figures, and the way by which they should be estimated is still under discussion. The inclusion of these indirect effects in LCA represents the next research challenges for LCA practitioners.

In fact, even though valuable improvements were achieved in determining the direct GHG emissions of bioenergy, a standard methodology for the indirect effects is still at a preliminary phase, and further research is needed. It is therefore predictable that future LCA studies will focus on reducing the uncertainties of these current key open issues (e.g., inclusion in the assessment of indirect land use change [LUC] effects and their amortization over time, estimation of bioenergy impacts on biodiversity, better determination of fertilizer induced emissions, and others). However, standardization in GHG balance accounting (also called carbon footprinting) of products is particularly perceived as urgent by policy makers, and the methodological standards provided by consultants and stakeholders try to address this need. A variety of policy objectives have motivated governments around the world to promote bioenergy and biofuels, on condition that a certain amount of GHG emission savings is achieved.

This means that legislation requires a standardized GHG accounting procedure encompassing the inclusion of indirect emissions in the life cycle of bioenergy, even if this topic is still in its scientific infancy. To cover this gap, several methodological standards have been proposed, as previously mentioned. In most of the cases, these guidelines tend to simplify or overlook concepts and issues of paramount importance, like indirect LUC effects and carbon storage in products. In addition, methodological standards usually limit the assessment to an extremely small number of indices and indicators. On one hand, these simplifications can make the overall assessment and interpretation of results easier, but on the other

104 Life Cycle Assessment

hand approximation and fixed approaches may have the drawback of misleading and inaccurate conclusions.

Therefore, the formulation of regulatory standards in the presence of scientific uncertainty may lead to inefficient or counterproductive methodologies. Finding a compromise is challenging, because a certain degree of simplicity and standardization in sustainability assessment of bioenergy systems is highly desirable nowadays, especially at a governmental and political level, where the best strategies for climate change mitigation should be put into practice as soon as possible. An example of this quandary can be found in the current situation for the Clean Development Mechanism (CDM), a trading framework established by the Kyoto Protocol that allows emission-reducing projects in developing countries to earn and sell carbon credits. Despite the high growth in transportation biofuel investment and research in recent years, not a single project on transportation biofuels has been successfully registered under the CDM (Bird et al., 2008). One of the most important reasons for such an astonishing result is the lack of standard methodologies for assessing GHG balance from agricultural and forest land. In fact, while the CDM focuses on the effects of individual projects, the land use issues discussed in this chapter can hardly be attributed to a single activity but tend to be the results of macroeconomic developments. Standardization in the inclusion of indirect effects in LCA may also give the possibility to establish LUC policies aiming at mitigating climate change. In fact, while deforestation and decrease of Soil Organic Carbon (SOC) are threatens for climate change, suitable land use policies may even lead to the opposite effect, given the large potential of GHG mitigation provided by CO_2 sequestration in terrestrial.

10.10 LCA IN HIGHER EDUCATION

In this study, expert panels were conducted based on the five-step nominal group technique as described in Potter et al. (2004) and Harvey and Holmes (2012) to build stepwise consensus on the learning outcomes and achievable competencies in higher education on LCA. Forum for Sustainability through Life Cycle Innovation (FSLCI) had invited about 40 internationally recognized universities and academic institutions and announced open expert panel workshops at the 2017 and 2019 Life Cycle Management Conferences. Three semi-structured expert panels were conducted in Luxembourg in 2017, at the University of Bordeaux in 2019, and due to the COVID-19 crisis online in 2020. The experts, who participated in the panels represented the following stakeholders of higher education in LCA:

- Université de Bordeaux and the engineering school Bordeaux INP (France), where LCA is integrated into general and professional bachelor studies (natural sciences and engineering), in master's (chemistry and engineering), and PhD programs.
- Technical University of Denmark (DTU), which is an engineering university, where sustainability assessment and life cycle thinking are introduced to all

Future Challenges for LCA

students at BSc, MSc, and PhD levels (via mandatory courses), and where LCA has been comprehensively taught at MSc level for the past 20 years.

- Technische Universität Darmstadt, where the Chair of Material Flow Management and Resource Economy provides LCA teaching for bachelor (environmental and civil engineering), master (various engineering and material sciences) and PhD programs.
- Pforzheim University's business school (Germany), where LCA is the core content of a master program provided by the Institute for Industrial Ecology and major part of several PhD studies.
- Université de Sherbrooke (Canada), where the Inter- disciplinary Research Laboratory in Life Cycle Assessment and Circular Economy (LIRIDE) integrated the concept of sustainable development and life cycle thinking into the bachelor, master, and PhD programs (various disciplines of engineering).
- Solent University, Southampton (UK) where LCA is taught as an integrated topic across the engineering bachelor's programs and several PhD studies.
- The Zurich University of Applied Sciences (ZHAW), where life cycle thinking and the application of LCA results are integrated in various bachelor and master's programs (engineering and life sciences) and in depth LCA competences are taught in a specific LCA minor for environmental engineers (Bachelor) and in advanced LCA courses in the master's program on natural resource sciences.

10.11 DATA INVENTORY AND LCA SOFTWARE

It was necessary to create databases of elements and materials to create LCA analysis and to speed up and simplify the entire process. The database must be updated according to production development, application of new and more effective ways of mining and extraction, and many other factors. Databases should be locally divided, due to non-uniform production process methods and conditions in each country. For simplifying and effective LCA performing, software tools for model processing need to be developed. It is necessary to collect all information about used materials, their volumes, information about technical building equipment, operational information, and so forth. In software that information is track down and summarized. Databases then generate results. With these tools the complete process of analysis is simplified and more accessible. In the brief time since the emergence of LCA, many software tools have been developed, including the following:

1. Athena (Canada), www.athenasmi.org/our-software-data/impact-estimator
2. BEES (USA), www.nist.gov/el/economics/BEESSoftware.cfm
3. Bilan Produit ADEME (France), www.base-impacts.ademe.fr/bilan-produit
4. General Carbon Footprint (UK), www.carbonfootprint.com/
5. eToolLCD (Australia), http://etoolglobal.com
6. ECOSOFT (Austria), www.ibo.at/en/ecosoft.htm

106   Life Cycle Assessment

7. GaBi (Germany), www.gabi-software.com/
8. GreenCalc+ (The Netherlands), www.greencalc.com
9. LEGEP (Germany), www.legep-software.de
10. OneClickLCA(Finland),www.oneclicklca.com/green-building-software/
11. Open LCA (Germany), www.openlca.org/General
12. SimaPro (The Netherlands), www.pre-sustainability.com/

10.12   CONCLUSION

The most important application of LCA is learning and understanding fundamental problems caused by products and systems from cradle to grave—that is,
from raw materials to recycling and waste removal, respectively. But the modern software offers immense help in performing LCA which were not available
at decades ago, it should not however replace the collection of original primary
data through system analysis tools for selection and an explanation of impact
categories.

LCA is a central tool that incorporates various environmental parameters with
this system considering the entire life cycle from cradle to grave of the product.
The present society has undergone a paradigm shift from environment to sustainability, which doesn't only focus on environmental impacts but also preserves the
natural resources. It rather three triangle points like environment, economy, and
social values for which society needs to find balance, Now this sustainable dice
accepted by all stakeholders is a guiding principle for both corporate strategy
and public policy making, however the biggest challenge for most organizations
remain the real and substantial of the sustainability concept and implementing it.
The challenges before sustainability goal is the measurement of various parameters' performance especially for product and process. The LCA is the only tool
available which helps identifying various steps required for the environmental
social justice and economic prosperity without limiting the ability of future generations to meet their needs. This holistic, systematic, and rigorous technique
is preferred when it comes to compiling assessing information about potential
environmental impacts.

The life cycle assessment study quantifies environmental impact across the
wide range of indicators but always includes a full carbon footprint. In LCA with
carbon footprint, two systems are highly complementary. But LCA study combined with the design principal of climate change opens up an opportunity for
CE. But the ultimate CE also looks at the neutralization of material but is more
high-level view which considers the idea like synergizing with two industries;
one of industries waste can be consumed in another industry as an alternate raw
material as blending material for the product. One can deal the three key issues in
sustainability by combining to form ultimate triangle between life cycle assessment cradle to cradle in CE. Some companies are already putting these ideas in
good use. This is where C2C stands apart from the conventional thinking around
sustainability. While in LCA is a steady focus primarily on reducing the negative impact of a product. Sustainable performance can be maximized by bringing

Future Challenges for LCA 107

together reliable data of quantitative LCA of two process or products. This concept is used wider for synergizing with two industries, integrating with CE. It is minimize the environmental impacts land move towards positive environmental footprint. Though there are many challenges to upgrade the technology, by using AI, Cloud, and blockchain in operational facilitator for data evaluation, inventory, and interpretation of various impacts.

Bibliography

1. Society of Environmental Toxicology and Chemistry (SETAC): *Summary Report on Life Cycle Assessment and Conceptually Related Programmes.* https:// https://www.setac.org.
2. Guinee, J.B.: *Handbook on Life Cycle Assessment—Operational Guide to the ISO Standards*, Kluwer Academic Publishers, AH Dordrecht, the Netherlands, 2002.
3. Udo de Haes, H.A., Jolliet, O., et al.: *Towards Best Available Methods for Life Cycle Impact Assessment.* Society of Environmental Toxicology and Chemistry (SETAC), 2002. ISBN 1-880661-64-6.
4. Pati, S.N., Roy, B.S., Raina, S., Veeramani, H.: Sustainable environment for Indian cement industry—A life cycle approach. *8th NCB International Seminar on Cement and Building Materials Proceedings*, Vol. 2, VII, pp. 48–56, 2003.
5. Pati, S.N., Roy, B.S., Raina, S.: Dimension to environmental management for cement industry—Life cycle approach. *CMA International Seminar on Cost Effective in Cement Manufacture and Construction Technological and Management Options Proceedings*, Vol. 2, pp. 19–30, 2005.
6. Pati, S.N.: *A Life Cycle Approach for Cement Industry Awareness Programme on "Environment Statements, Including Environmental Auditing, Waste Minimization & Management System for Cement Industry".* CBRI, Roorkee Publication, March 16–18, pp. 10–27, 2005.
7. Pati, S.N.: How to use life cycle assessment in Indian cement industry. *National Workshop on Life Cycle Assessment for Cement Sector.* New Delhi: NCB Publication, pp. 1–60, May 18, 2005.
8. Pati, S.N.: Growth of Indian cement industry. *NCB-CMA Special Publication, Eighth NCB International Seminar on Cement and Building Materials.* New Delhi, India, p. 17, 18–21 November 2003.
9. Pati, S.N.: New dimension to environmental management integrating LCA and exergy accounting system. *IAEM National Conference on Innovative Approaches in the Management of Environment*, 49 p, 2003.
10. ISO 26000: *Guidance on Social Responsibility.* International Organization for Standardization, 2010.
11. UNEP/SETAC: *Life Cycle Management. A Business Guide to Sustainability. UNEP/SETAC Life Cycle Initiative.* UNEP, Paris, Companies that Commit to Green Policies Will Attract Consumers, 26 February 2007.
12. ISO 14047: *Examples of Application of ISO 14042.*
13. ISO 14049–2002: *Examples of ISO 14041.*
14. Finkbeiner, M., Schau, E., Lehmann, A., Traverso, M.: Towards life cycle sustainability assessment. *Sustainability* 2(10):3309–3322 (2010).
15. Pati, S.N.: *A Handbook on Corporate Sustainability*, Institute Of Directors Publication, New Delhi, 2012.
16. Pati, S.N.: *Adopt Life Cycle Assessment (LCA) for Sustainability Driving "Sustainable Business through Green Economy"*, IOD Publication, New Delhi, pp. 78–84, 2012.
17. EC-JRC.: *European Commission—Joint Research Centre—Institute for Environment and Sustainability: International Reference Life Cycle Data System (ILCD) Handbook—General Guide for Life Cycle Assessment—Detailed Guidance.* First edition March 2010. EUR 24708 EN. Publications Office of the European Union, Luxembourg, 2010.

18. Revised IPCC Guidelines for National Green House Gas Inventories: Reference Manual 1996. https://www.ipcc.ch/.
19. Ekvall, T., Azapagic, A., Finnveden, G., et al.: Attributional and consequential LCA in the ILCD handbook. *Int. J. Life Cycle Assess.* 21:293–296 (2016).
20. ISO 14044: *Environmental Management—Life Cycle Assessment—Requirements and Guidelines.* International Organization for Standardization, Geneva, Switzerland, 2006.
21. National Building Code, *Bureau of Indian Standards*, 2005.
22. Garg, T.: *Green Building*, TERI, New Delhi, 14 October 2010.
23. Jolliet, O., Saadé-Sbeih, M., Shaked, S., Jolliet, A., Crettaz, P.: *Environmental Life Cycle Assessment*, CRC Press, 2016.
24. Klöpffer, W., Grahl, B.: *Life Cycle Assessment: A Guide to Best Practice*, Wiley-VCH, Weinheim, 2014.
25. Circular Economy Stahel, W.R.: *The Circular Economy: A User's Guide*, Routledge, 2019.
26. Ellen MacArthur Foundation & ARUP: *Circular Economy in Cities*, 2019. http://mava-foundation.org/wp-content/uploads/2019/01/EMF-Circular-economy-in-cities-preview-paper-1.pdf.
27. United Nations Development Programme: *Goal 11: Sustainable Cities and Communities*, 2019. www.undp.org/content/oslo-governance-centre/en/home/sustainable-development-goals/goal-11-sustainable-cities-and-communities.html.
28. Using Life Cycle Assessment to Achieve a Circular Economy. *Position Paper of the Life Cycle Initiative*, July 2020.
29. ISO 14040: *Environmental Management—Life Cycle Assessment—Principles and Framework.* International Organization for Standardization, Geneva, Switzerland, 2006.
30. ISO 14044: *Environmental Management—Life Cycle Assessment—Requirements and Guidelines.* International Organization for Standardization, Geneva, Switzerland, 2006.
31. Finkbeiner, M.: Product environmental footprint—breakthrough or breakdown for policy implementation of life cycle assessment? *Int. J. Life Cycle Assess.* 19:266–271 (2014). https://doi.org/10.1007/s11367-013-0678-x.
32. Frankl, P., Rubik, F.: *Life Cycle Assessment in Industry and Business. Adoption Patterns, Applications, and Implications*, IGARSS Int. J. Life Cycle Assess, Heidelberg, Germany, 2014, 2000, https://doi.org/10.1007/s13398-014-0173-7.2.
33. Galatola, M., Pant, R.: Reply to the editorial "product environmental footprint—breakthrough or breakdown for policy implementation of life cycle assessment?" Written by Prof. Finkbeiner. Int J Life Cycle Assess 19(2):266–271. *Int. J. Life Cycle Assess.* 19:1356–1360 (2014). https://doi.org/10.1007/s11367-014-0740-3.
34. Gonzalez, P., Sarkis, J., Adenso-Diaz, B.: Environmental management system certification and its influence on corporate practices. Evidence from the automotive industry. *Int. J. Oper. Prod. Manag.* 28:1021–1041 (2008).
35. Hanssen, O.J.: Status of life cycle assessment (LCA) activities in the Nordic region. *Int. J. Life Cycle Assess.* 4:262–262 (1999). https://doi.org/10.1007/BF02979177.
36. Heiskanen, E.: Managers' interpretations of LCA: Enlightenment and responsibility or confusion and denial? *Bus. Strateg. Environ.* 9:239–254 (2000).
37. Huang, E., Hunkeler, D.: *Life Cycle Analysis: Summary of a Fortune 500 Survey and a Japanese Comparison*, Vanderbilt University, 1995.
38. Johnson, M.P., Schaltegger, S.: Two decades of sustainability management tools for SMEs: How far have we come? *J. Small Bus. Manag.* 54(2):481–505 (2015). https://doi.org/10.1111/jsbm.12154.

Bibliography

39. Kurczewski, P.: Life cycle thinking in small and medium enterprises: The results of research on the implementation of life cycle tools in Polish SMEs-part 1: Background and framework. *Int. J. Life Cycle Assess.* 19(3):593–600 (2013).

40. Lewandowska, A., Kurczewski, P., Kulczycka, J., Joachimiak, K., Matuszak-Flejszman, A., Baumann, H., Ciroth, A.: LCA as an element in environmental management systems—comparison of conditions in selected organisations in Poland, Sweden and Germany: Part 1: Background and initial assumptions. *Int. J. Life Cycle Assess.* 18:472–480 (2013). https://doi.org/10.1007/s11367-012-0480-1.

41. Lewandowska, A., Matuszak-Flejszman, A.: Eco-design as a normative element of Environmental Management Systems—the context of the revised ISO 14001:2015. *Int. J. Life Cycle Assess.* 19:1794–1798 (2014). https://doi.org/10.1007/s11367-014-0787-1.

42. Lombardo, P.: Environmental management systems. In: Ahmed, K., ed. *Getting to Green: A Sourcebook of Pollution Management Policy Tools for Growth and Competitiveness,* World Bank, Washington, DC, 2012.

43. Meylan, G., Stauffacher, M., Krütli, P., et al.: Identifying stakeholders' views on the eco-efficiency assessment of a municipal solid waste management system. *J. Ind. Ecol.* 19(3):490–503 (2014). https://doi.org/10.1111/jiec.12192.

44. Nakano, K., Hirao, M.: Collaborative activity with business partners for improvement of product environmental performance using LCA. *J. Clean. Prod.* 19:1189–1197 (2011).

45. Schischke, K., Nissen, N.F., Sherry, J., et al.: Life cycle thinking in small and medium sized enterprises—status quo and strategic needs in the electronics sector. In: *Electronics Go Green,* Stuttgart, Germany, 2012.

46. Stewart, J.R., Collins, M.W., Anderson, R., Murphy, W.R.: Life cycle assessment as a tool for environmental management. *Clean Technol. Environ. Policy* 1:73–81 (1999).

47. Wenzel, H., Hauschild, M.Z., Alting, L.: Environmental assessment of products. In: *Vol. 1—Methodology, Tools and Case Studies in Product Development.* Kluwer Academic Publishers, Hingham, p. 544, 1997. ISBN 0 412 80800 5.

48. Witczak, J., Kasprzak, J., Klos, Z., et al.: Life cycle thinking in small and medium enterprises: The results of research on the implementation of life cycle tools in Polish SMEs-part 2: LCA related aspects. *Int. J. Life Cycle Assess.* 19(1):891–900 (2014).

49. Zackrisson, M., Rocha, C., Christiansen, K., Jarnehammar, A.: Stepwise environmental product declarations: Ten SME case studies. *J. Clean. Prod.* 16:1872–1886 (2008).

50. Curran, M.A., Mann, M., Norris, G.: The international workshop on electricity data for life cycle inventories. *J. Clean. Prod.* 13(8):853–862 (2005).

51. Curran, M.A.: Assessing environmental impacts of biofuels using life cycle-based approaches. *Manag. Environ. Qual.* 24(1):34–52 (2013).

52. De Schrynmakers, P.: Life cycle thinking in the aluminium industry. *Int. J. Life Cycle Assess.* 14(Suppl 1):S2–S5 (2009).

53. Ekvall, T., Tillman, A.-M., Molander, S.: Normative ethics and methodology for life cycle assessment. *J. Clean Prod.* 13(13–14):1225–12334 (2005).

54. Finnveden, G., Hauschild, M.Z., Ekvall, T., Guinée, J., Heijungs, R., Hellweg, S., Koehler, A., Pennington, D., Suh, S.: Recent developments in life cycle assessment. *J. Environ. Manag.* 91:1–21 (2009).

55. Margni, M., Curran, M.A.: Life cycle impact assessment. In: Curran, M.A., ed. *Life Cycle Assessment Handbook: A Guide for Environmentally Sustainable Products,* Chapter 4, Scrivener Publishing, Beverly, 2012.

56. Notarnicola, B., Tassielli, G., Renzulli, P.: Modeling the GRI-food industry with life cycle assessment. In: Curran, M.A., ed. *Life Cycle Assessment Handbook: A*

Guide for Environmentally Sustainable Products, Chapter 7, Scrivener Publishing, Beverly, 2012.

57. Ngo, A.K.: Environmental accountability: A new paradigm for world trade is emerging. In: Curran, M.A., ed. *Life Cycle Assessment Handbook: A Guide for Environmentally Sustainable Products*, Chapter 24, Scrivener Publishing, Beverly, 2012.

58. Searchinger, T., Heimlich, R., et al.: Use of US cropland for biofuels increases greenhouse gases through emissions from land-use change. *Science* 319(5867):1238–1240 (2008).

59. Workshop Report, Society Of Environmental Toxicology And Chemistry (SETAC) Smugglers Notch, Vermont: A technical framework for life cycle assessments. In: Fava, J., Denison, R., et al. eds., 1990.

60. SETAC: Guidelines for life-cycle assessment: A code of practice. In: Consoli, F., Allen, D., et al., eds. *Society of Environmental Toxicology and Chemistry (SETAC)*, SETAC, Brussels, 1993.

61. UNEP: *Global Guidance Principles for Life Cycle Assessment Databases: A Basis for Greener Processes and Products*, United Nations Environment Programme, Paris UNEP/SETAC, 2011.

62. Valdivia, S., Ugaya, C.M.L., Sonnemann, G., Hildenbrand, J., eds.: *Towards a Life Cycle Sustainability Assessment-making Informed Choices on Products*,UNEP, Paris. ISBN 978-92-807-3175-0.

63. US EPA: *An Examination of EPA Risk Assessment Principles and Practices, EPA/100/B-04/00*, Office of the Science Advisor, Washington, DC, 2004.

64. US EPA: Guidance to facilitate decisions for sustainable nanotechnology, EPA/600/R-11/107. *US Environmental Protection Agency*, Office of Research & Development, Cincinnati, 2011.

65. Hauschild, M.Z., Huijbregts, M.A.J.: *Life Cycle Impact Assessment*, Springer Publishers, 2015.

66. Guinée, J.B., Gorrée, M., Heijungs, R., Huppes, G., Kleijn, R., Koning, A. de, Oers, L. van, Wegener Sleeswijk, A., Suh, S., Udo de Haes, H.A.: *Hand Book on Life Cycle Assessment-Operational Guide to the ISO Standards*, Kluwer Academic Publishers, 2004.

67. Sonnemann, G., Margni, M.: *Life Cycle Management*, Springer Publishers, 2015.

68. Benoît, C., Norris, G.A., Valdivia, S., Ciroth, A., Moberg, A., Bos, U., Prakash, S., Ugaya, C., Beck, T.: The guidelines for social life cycle assessment of products: Just in time! *Int. J. Life Cycle Assess.* 15(2):156–163 (2010).

69. Capitano, C., Traverso, M., Rizzo, G., Finkbeiner, M.: Life cycle sustainability assessment: An implementation to marble products. *Proceedings of the LCM 2011 Conference*, Berlin, 29–31 August 2011, 2011.

70. Cavanagh, J., Frame, B., Lennox, J.: The sustainability assessment model (SAM): Measuring sustainable development performance. *Australas. J. Environ. Manag.* 13:142–145 (2006).

71. Elkington, J.: *Cannibals with Forks: The Triple Bottom Line in 21st Century Businesses*, New Society Publishers, Gabriola Island, 1998.

72. Finkbeiner, M., Schau, E., Lehmann, A., Traverso, M.: Towards life cycle sustainability assessment. *Sustainability* 2(10):3309–3322 (2010). https://doi.org/10.3390/su2103309.

73. Guinée, J.B., Gorrée, M., Heijungs, R., Huppes, G., Kleijn, R., Koning, A. de, Oers, L. van, Wegener Sleeswijk, A., Suh, S., Udo de Haes, H.A., Bruijn, H. de, Duin, R. van, Huijbregts, M.A.J.: *Handbook on Life Cycle Assessment. Operational Guide to the ISO Standards. I: LCA in Perspective. IIa: Guide. IIb: Operational Annex. III: Scientific Background*. Kluwer Academic Publishers, Dordrecht, 2002.

Bibliography

74. Halog, A., Manik, J.: Advancing integrated systems modelling framework for life cycle sustainability assessment. *Sustainability* 3(2):469–499 (2011).
75. Hardi, P., Semple, P.: The dashboard of sustainability—From a metaphor to an operational set of indices. *5th International Conference on Social Science Methodology*, Cologne, Germany, 2000.
76. UNEP/SETAC: *Life Cycle Management. A Business Guide to Sustainability. UNEP/SETAC Life Cycle Initiative*, UNEP, Paris, 2007.
77. Valdivia, S., Ciroth, A., Ugaya, C., Lu, B., Sonnemann, G., Fontes, J., Alvarado, C., Tischhauser, S.: A UNEP/ SETAC toolbox for LC sustainability assessment of products. *Proceedings of the 9th International Conference on EcoBalance*, Tokyo, 2010.
78. Ghosh, S.N.: *Advances in Cement Technology*, Second Edition Tech Book International, New Delhi, 2002. http://www.technobooks.com.
79. Duda, W.H.: *Cement Data Book*, Volume 3, French & European Publications Inc, New York, 2013.
80. Peray, K.E.: *The Rotary Cement Kiln*, Chemical Publishing Book – Gloucester, MA 01930, Paperback 2002.
81. EC-JRC.: *European Commission—Joint Research Centre—Institute for Environment and Sustainability: International Reference Life Cycle Data System (ILCD) Handbook—General Guide for Life Cycle Assessment—Detailed Guidance*. First edition March 2010. EUR 24708 EN. Publications Office of the European Union, Luxembourg, 2010.
82. EC-JRC: *European Commission—Joint Research Centre—Institute for Environment and Sustainability: International Reference Life Cycle Data System (ILCD) Handbook—Recommendations for Life Cycle Impact Assessment in the European Context—Based on Existing Environmental Impact Assessment Models and Factors*. First edition 2011, EUR 24571 EN. Publication Office of the European Union, Luxemburg, 2011.
83. Miller, S.A.: The role of cement service-life on the efficient use of resources. *Environ. Res. Lett.* 15(2):024004 (2020).
84. Sanchez, S., Cancio, Y., Sanchez, I.R., Martirena, J.F., Rosa, E.R., Habert, G.: Sustainability assessment in Cuban Cement Sector—A methodological approach. *Earth Environ. Sci.* 323:012128 (2019).
85. Nigri, E.M., Rocha, S.D.F., Filho, E.R.: Portland cement: On application of life cycle assessment. *Manag. Dev.* 8(December):167 (2010).
86. Seyler, C., Hellweg, S., Monteil, M., Hungerbuhler, K.: Life cycle inventory for use of waste solvent as fuel substitute in the cement industry—A multi-input allocation model. *Int. J. Life Cycle Assess.* 10(2):120–130 (2005).
87. Hopkins, J.M., Busch, J., Purnell, P., Zwirner, O., Velis, C.A., Brown, A., Hahladakis, J., Iacovidou, E.: Fully of the total environment modelling for sustainability assessment of resource recovery from wastes. *Science* 612:613–624 (2018).
88. Gusano, D.G., Herrear, I., Garrain, D., Lechon, Y., Cabal, H.: Life cycle assessment of the Spanish cement industry: Implementation of environmental friendly solutions. *Clean Technol. Environ. Policy.* 17:59–73 (2015).
89. Rosyid, A., Boedisantoso, R., Iswara, A.P.: Environmental impact studied using life cycle assessment on cement industry. *Earth Environ. Sci.* 506:012024 (2020).
90. Horakova, A., Schreiberova, H., Broukalova, I., Fladr, J.: Decrease of cement production environmental burden—life cycle assessment. *Earth Environ. Sci.* 290:012048 (2019).
91. Klöpffer, W., Curran, M.A., eds.: *LCA Compendium—The Complete World of Life Cycle Assessment Series*, Springer, 2016.

92. Goglio, P., Williams, A., Balta-Ozkan, N., Harris, N.R.P., Williamson, P., Huisingh, D., Zhang, Z., Tavoni, M.: Advances and challenges of life cycle assessment (LCA) of greenhouse gas removal technologies to fight climate change. *J. Clean. Prod.* 244(October):118896 (2019).
93. Finkbeiner, M., ed.: *Towards Life Cycle Sustainability Management*, Springer, 2011.
94. Jolliet, O., Saadé-Sbeih, M., Shaked, S., Jolliet, A., Crettaz, P.: *Environmental Life Cycle Assessment*, CRC Press, 2016.
95. Horne, R., Grant, T., Verghese, K.: *Life Cycle Assessment*, CSIRO Publishing, 2009.
96. Finkbeiner, M., ed.: *Special Types of Life Cycle Assessment*, Springer, 2016.
97. Klöpffer, W., Grahl, B.: *Life Cycle Assessment: A Guide to Best Practice*, Wiley-VCH, Weinheim, 2014.
98. Pati, S.N., Salahuddin, M.: *Life Cycle Assessment (LCA) Studies of Construction Industry*. Published by MOEF, and NCB 1–40 p, 2012.
99. *Why Take a Life Cycle Approach*, UNEP Publication, 2004.
100. *Guidelines for Social Life Cycle Assessment of Products*, UNEP Publication, 2009.
101. *Guidance on Organizational Life Cycle Assessment*, UNEP Publication, 2015.
102. *LCA of Building Materials—Impact Assessment and Interpretation in the Building Materials Industry, for German Building Materials Association*, University of Stuttgart, German, 2000.
103. Behzad, E., Sarkisb, J., Lewisc, K., Behdadd, S.: Blockchain for the future of sustainable supply chain management in Industry 4.0. *Resour. Conserv. Recy.* 163(5):105064 (2020).
104. Thonemann, N., Schulte, A., Maga, D.: How to conduct prospective life cycle assessment for emerging technologies? A systematic review and methodological guidance. *Sustainability* 12:1192 (2020). https://doi.org/10.3390/su12031192.
105. Groen, E.A., Bokkers, E.A., Heijungs, R., Boer, I.J.M.: Methods for global sensitivity analysis in life cycle assessment. *Int. J. Life Cycle Assess.* 22:1125–1137 (2017).
106. Lu, H., Masanet, E., Price, L.: *Evaluation of life-cycle assessment studies of Chinese cement production: Challenges and opportunities*. Proceedings of the ACEEE Summer Study on Energy Efficiency in Industry, 2009. www.iscp.org.cn/clcm2008en/default.aspx.
107. *Towards A Life Cycle Sustainability Assessment—Making Informed Choices on Products*, UNEP Publication, UNEP/SETAC Life Cycle Initiative, 2011.

Index

Note: Page numbers in *italics* indicate figures and page numbers in **bold** indicate tables.

A

abiotic resources, 77
acidification potential, 36
afforestation, 78
allocation procedure, 31
attributional life cycle assessment (ALCA), 64
awareness of life cycle thinking, 97

B

building
    construction, 93
    demolition, 94
    maintenance, 94
    operation, 93

C

capacity building, 58
carbon capture and utilization, 102
carbon capture through algae, 74
carbon neutrality, 102
carbon sequestration, 73
case studies
    Brazil, 87
    China, 90
    Czech Republic, 89
    Germany, 91
    India, 92–93
    Indonesia, 88
    Spain, 86
    Switzerland, 88
    UK, 85
    USA, 85
chronological development of LCA, 20, **21**
circular economy, 2, 10, 101
classification, 39
climate change, 9, 71
consequential life cycle assessment, 65
consistency check, 83
consumer perspective, 69
continual improvement, 17
corporate level, 69
corporate sustainability, 3
COVID-19, 16
critical review, 84

D

data collection, 56
data source, 28
data variability and consistency, 28
degradation of forest, 1
details of commercial buildings, **41**
documentation and review, 57

E

ecotoxicity, 76
environmental mechanism, 72
environmental product declaration, 84
environment data, *13*
environment management system, 9, 11, 12, *13*
eutrophication, 76
evaluation, 82
exergy assimilation, 100
extended boundary, *23*
extension, 15

F

factor to consider, 16
framework, 21
functional unit, 30

G

globalization, 98
global movement, 9, *10*
goal and scope, 25, 26
greenhouse gas, 35
GWP, 35

H

human toxicity, 77

I

impact assessment, 31, **40**
impact assessment of commercial buildings, **42**
impact categories, **32**

115

Index

impact of blended cement, **33**
implementation, 14
industrial activities, 1
industrial unit, 68
input and output data, 57
integration and harmonization, 67, 99
international standards, 14
interpretation, 38, 83
inventory analysis, 26

L

land use, 37, 78
LCA in higher education, 104
LCA software, 105
life cycle analysis, 4
life cycle and sustainability system, *51*
life cycle assessment, 19, *24*, 43
life cycle costing, 44
life cycle impact categories, **40**
life cycle inventories, 55
life cycle sustainability assessment,
        49, *50*
life cycle thinking, 1, **22**, *24*, 63
life cycle tools, 43
limitations, 34

M

material balance, **28**
mitigation of climate change, 98

N

normalization, 37

O

organizational life cycle assessment, 51
ozone formation, 74

P

process flow, 29
product alternatives, **33**
product environmental footprint, 84

R

rebooting, 15
reduction measure of GHG, 72
reduction of carbon and water footprints, 15
reorientation, 16
re-philosophy, 2
resource depletion, 37

S

sensitivity check, 82
small and medium sized enterprises, 68
social life cycle assessment, 45
sustainability for construction industry, *95*
sustainable consumption and production, 103
sustainable development, *13*
sustainable future, 16, 17
system boundaries, 30

U

uncertainties, 34
uncertainty analysis, 38

V

validation, 29

W

water use, 79
WCED, 3
worship of nature, 1
WRI, 6

Printed in the United States
by Baker & Taylor Publisher Services